THE LEARNING PROCESS
FOR MANAGERS

Other Books by the Same Author

PRIMITIVE PROPERTY

CRIME

CRIME, CRIMINALS AND CRIMINAL JUSTICE

CRIME AND SOCIETY

DYNAMICS OF LEARNING

EMPLOYEE COUNSELING

LEARNING THROUGH DISCUSSION

THE TEACHING-LEARNING PROCESS

THE LEARNING PROCESS
FOR MANAGERS

by Nathaniel Cantor

PROFESSOR OF SOCIOLOGY
UNIVERSITY OF BUFFALO

HARPER & BROTHERS PUBLISHERS

NEW YORK

CONTENTS

PREFACE

It is encouraging to watch the recent and present movement in manager development programs. Some confusion and uncertainty are inevitable in the planning of such programs. There is no agreement on the objectives of such programs, on the contents or the methods of communicating the materials.

Many of the training programs now in use, even those of the leading companies, are part of a fad for training—a bandwagon approach. Expensive training directors are hired and programs initiated before objectives are outlined. Many executives and staff managers are caught up in training without much understanding of the development of true *managerial direction* or how it is to be communicated.

This study is one person's effort to bring a bit more order into the solving of these problems. I try first to describe what the function of a manager is and then to explore the teaching-learning process through which the goals of a program may be communicated.

I should like to express my appreciation to the Committee of Allocation of Research Funds of the University of Buffalo for financial help in gathering materials for this study.

Much of my own learning occurred through discussions with members of many workshops which I was privileged to conduct and with staff members of the American Telephone and Telegraph Company, DuPont de Nemours and Company, Canadian International Paper Company, St. Regis Paper Company, Western Electric Corporation, and the Champion Paper and Fibre Company. I also wish to thank my publishers for many suggestions which I am sure have improved this study.

June 1957   NATHANIEL CANTOR

PART 1

THE FUNCTION OF MANAGERS

"The greatest weakness in the Federal government's personnel is inexpert managerial direction."

The Hoover Commission

1

THE MAKING OF A MANAGER:
MAN OR MANUAL?

This study deals with the development of managers.[1] It is concerned with the manager's responsibility for developing the potential of those for whom he is responsible. Traditionally, the criterion of sound management practices was based upon productivity. This criterion may be sound in relation to efficient production, increased sales, and lower costs. In the latter cases, the manager is developing or improving one's *technical* know-how.

We are not concerned with that aspect of the problem of management development. We assume that managers already possess the required technical skills or can, in time, acquire the necessary technical competence. We are interested, rather, in how well a manager can assist those who are directly associated with him and whom he directs in becoming more creative in their own job performance. We are interested in expert managerial direction, the most serious weakness in industrial personnel.

Productivity depends upon hard work. Fortunately, the development of mechanical production processes and the multiplication of power tools have lessened and conserved the workers' physical effort. Incentives, whether in the form of bonuses, vacations, guaranteed wages, or pensions, have generally not led to increased productivity. The division of labor and the increasing use of automatic processes tend to remove interest and challenge in the worker's job. More than ever there is a need for the ideas of employees and the widening of their interests on the job.

This brings us to the intangible aspects of managing, the shaping of the attitudes of fellow workers. Technical management skills are essential. The troublesome problems, however, arise because managers often do not know how to help their subordinates. "Call it what you will, there are certain intangibles in a man's sense of values, his attitude, his self-appraisal, which get communicated and affect his relationships with others."[2]

Many top managers do not know how to help their subordinates but will agree that personal leadership is the most effective production incentive. Yet subordinates are not likely to talk with superiors about matters which concern them most. They talk about what they think the superior would like to hear. Important conflicts and trouble spots down the line are rarely revealed to the superior.[3]

The mushrooming of management development programs in the last fifteen years is an indication of the genuine concern of companies with the area of their managers' attitudes and values.

WHAT KIND OF PROGRAM

Management development programs have become an integral part of American industry's effort to develop executive and supervisory leadership. There is much uncertainty and disagreement regarding their nature, what the objectives should be, the content, methods, and leadership of the programs.

Efforts to develop managers vary from the ambitious programs of schools of business administration, for senior executives with many years of experience, to the weekly letters to managers from "service organizations." A few of our well-known corporations send their junior executives to college to receive a liberal arts, humanities orientation. Many managers attend various state and national management association conferences, which last from one meeting to an entire week.

A case study method is employed by many companies.[4] Each participant reads the description of a problem which has arisen in an organization. The problem is usually not clearly stated, but is found in a series of complexities that characterize any involved situation in which people and issues are all tangled up. The participants are expected to locate the central issue and to decide upon an action, even when all the facts are not available. Supporters of the case study method of management development suppose that the participants will discover how complex problems can be, that there are alternative solutions as well as different approaches, that the participants will learn from each other, and that, if there are generalizations which can help one in resolving problems in industry and business, they can be learned through discussion of actual cases.

Many corporations still rely upon job rotation as the best form of management development. If an executive moves from one position or area of responsibility to another, his understanding of the organization's problems will presumably be broadened. Thus a manager might move from engineering to production to sales to advertising and then into manufacturing or perhaps research. It is questionable that a manager acquires new insight into attitudes in a familiar setting of his company.

Role playing is another form of management development. In this situation the participants take turns in observing each other act out, in an artificial setting, responses to problematic situations that occur in the industrial or business setting. The actors often switch roles, thereby being given the opportunity to experience the feeling of the one on the receiving end. The audience observes and evaluates the efforts of the actors. It is supposed that insight is thus gained.[5]

Some companies feel that the best way to develop managers is to have a senior executive take a subordinate under his own wing and guide him during day to day contacts. This is a widely accepted form of management development although it is not formally recognized as a basic method. Superior and subordinate managers who work together and discuss their problems are counseling each other.

Our primary purpose here is not to pass judgment upon the relative merits or disadvantages of the various programs employed in executive development. Our purpose is rather to point out that no one of these approaches necessarily touches the key problem which is, how does a manager gain insight into the kinds of uses he makes of himself, in relation to his work responsibilities and in relation to the people with whom he works?

No one method can accomplish the full job nor will any

method fail to provide some value to a manager who is willing to learn. We are dealing here with the most likely chance, assuming limits of time and money, and the most effective ways of helping managers to develop.

There are as many kinds of programs as there are corporations conducting them. No two are alike. Each organization is, so to speak, on its own, trying to find a sound program for developing a corps of managers.

There seems to be a dearth of staff consultants or personnel managers who possess sufficient insight to structure developmental programs or to lead them. This should surprise no one. There is almost no place where one can obtain the kinds of background required for managerial development. Indeed no one is sure what that background should consist of.[6]

I have examined scores of training programs which describe the content, objectives, and techniques to attain the goals. I have been struck by the fact that any given corporation or national association rarely continues into a second year with the same program. Again, this may be desirable experimentation reflecting a desire to learn and develop.

The general dissatisfaction currently felt by staff people responsible for such programs is a good sign. Those who are most serious about building meaningful programs seem to be the most dissatisfied. One of the difficulties is the lack of knowledge about this complex area of developing skills in directing the development of others. Furthermore, it is unlikely that there would be wide agreement on the characteristics of a creative manager.

When one deals with a program for manager development there are unrecognized teaching-learning assumptions which must be made clear, skills which must be analyzed, objectives which must be specifically defined, and the functions of a manager which must be clarified.

No one can present the knowledge or the experience which could *reliably* support *the* program for the development of managers. There are many approaches, but they will all have one thing in common. Any meaningful, genuine program cannot rest upon gimmicks, techniques, formulae, rules, handbooks, or manuals. The way to develop excellent managers is the same way used in becoming an excellent person. In brief, whatever program is planned to help in the discovery and improvement of managerial talent and potential, that program must help the participant to learn *to use himself* in the quality of his performance. Using others, employing tricks or formulae, exercising power or authority, telling others, and dominating subordinates are escapes from disciplining oneself, as we shall see. Some students agree with the view of Professor Myles L. Mace that "the most effective way of providing for the growth and development of people in manufacturing organizations is through the conscious coaching of subordinates by their immediate superiors."[7]

Robert C. Sampson does not deny the contribution of many formal training programs. He thinks they are fine as supplementary training "but that the primary task must be done on the job—that is, on the man's regular job." He realizes that what is needed "is to put *qualified* staff men in a new role—that of catalytic agents, so to speak, for executive development on the job."[8] (Italics mine.)

Unfortunately Mr. Mace does not indicate how the superiors are to acquire the skills and competence to coach and

Mr. Sampson does not tell us where the qualified staff men are to be found. Unquestionably, there are executives and staff men who possess superior understanding and the skills to communicate it, but such high competence is rare. There are too few with enough insight and teaching skill to develop the hundreds and thousands of managers who are needed now and who must be replaced in the future.

One of the most effective ways to become a professional manager is to join in conference with a small group of other managers who want to learn and to explore their organizational responsibilities and duties.

What characterizes a skilled manager has been the central theme of many workshops led by me for the past ten years. My experiences with hundreds of industrial and personnel managers, executives, and training directors who have participated in these intensive workshops have stimulated me to undertake this study.

The best way to gain insight into the problems of skilled leadership is to participate actively in such workshops. Next best, perhaps, is to closely observe through a written record what occurred during these workshops. The reader, so to speak, is present as an observer, listening to what is happening.

Mere "reading" is not enough. The reader's effort in trying to read between the lines, in testing his present beliefs and feelings against the changing beliefs of others, illuminates, modifies, or alters one's convictions.

No reader need agree with my views or the conclusions of the participants. Every reader, it is hoped, will discover something to challenge him so that after a careful study of this volume he will experience new insights into his own behavior as a person and as a manager. If he does, he will discover better ways to relate to his associates and subordinates, and thus become a more skilled manager, as well as a more sensitive and creative human being.

Every normal person wants to improve the quality of his living experience, to express himself, to feel good about himself and others. The development of a manager is essentially the development of the person. The quality of management performance cannot be separated from the quality of the people who are managers. The man, not the printed manual, makes the manager.

What develops the man? How does one achieve insight? No one knows the answers. There are good clues which have been discovered and which will be explored in subsequent chapters. One does *not* gain insight by being given answers or by being told. In a sense, then, trying to present what occurs in the learning process through a volume such as this seems to contradict the view that one does not learn anything vitally significant by listening or reading or by being given answers.

The contradiction is only apparent. There is no real contradiction since this study does not pretend or intend to give the reader insight. The reader presumably has come to this volume because of a prior genuine interest in management development. The material to be presented has been gathered through my experiences with hundreds of others who have shared these interests. I suppose the reader, too, wants to discover something for himself. These chapters, then, are intellectual statements or analytic descriptions of living processes.

Necessarily much of what occurs has to be left out. The data have to be frozen to be described. The reader must supply his own vital transfusions so that the intellectual substance becomes alive for him. This study is an instrument. The reader must perform upon it.

NOTES

1. The term "manager" as used throughout this book refers to anyone who is given supervisory responsibility. In this sense the first-line supervisors are considered managers. From the point of view of senior executives, junior executives or supervisors may be considered as employees. The context will make clear which status is being discussed.

2. O. A. Ohmann, "How to Increase Your Own Administrative Effectiveness," Edward C. Bursk (ed.), *How to Increase Executive Effectiveness* (Cambridge, Mass: Harvard University Press, 1953), p. 141-42.

3. Chris Argyris, *Executive Leadership and Appraisal of the Manager in Action* (New York: Harper & Brothers, 1953), p. 108-10.

4. *The Case Method of the Harvard Business School*, edited by Malcolm P. McNair (New York: McGraw-Hill Book Co., 1954).

5. Norman R. F. Maier, Allen R. Solem, Ayesha A. Maier, *Supervisory and Executive Development, A Manual for Role Playing* (New York: John Wiley and Sons, 1957).

6. In Peter Drucker, *The Practice of Management* (New York: Harper and Brothers, 1954), we find the beginnings of a clear statement and a fine analysis. There is little to be found, however, regarding how one *becomes* a skilled manager.

7. M. L. Mace, *The Growth and Development of Executives* (Cambridge, Mass: Harvard University Press, 1950), p. 107.

8. Robert C. Sampson, "Train Executives While They Work," *Harvard Business Review*, November-December, 1953, p. 43-44.

II

INDUSTRY AS A SOCIAL SYSTEM

EVERY large industrial organization is a bureaucracy. The formal organization chart indicates the centralization of control, the levels of authority, and the differentiation of function of the personnel. The line organization on the chart reveals who takes and who gives orders.

The formation of policy and the exercise of discretion are generally confined to groups of managers and supervisors who are appointed. They determine the different qualifications for different positions. Continuity of function is provided for; it is the position and not the individual that continues.

The formal chart, however, does not produce goods. It merely describes the anatomy or structure of the organization. There is another set of informal activities, namely, the processes of interaction and communication between the people who produce, sell, and distribute the goods. Even in the case of an automatically operated factory someone has to make decisions and push buttons. People in interaction are responsible for producing goods. It is naively supposed that the function of an industry is to produce goods through paying people a salary or wages. The traditional answer to the question of why people work, namely, "to get money," is too simple. The efficient production of goods is not merely a matter of formal organization by management and paying wages for work performed. Research has illuminated what the demands of workers are. Industrial plants are not merely factories where people produce goods for wages. They are also communities where people seek to express and to satisfy social needs.

The formal charts of a company which list the duties, functions, and responsibilities of various executives, supervisors, and employees do not indicate *the way* in which they will be carried out. People are not machines. Few rules are ever rigidly applied. Every group, every department, develops its own peculiar informal practices and routines. These informal practices and the modification of formal rules must be appreciated and accepted if the cooperation of employees is to be won. Rules cannot be arbitrarily imposed without lowering morale. They must be understood and accepted by the people affected by the regulations if efficient performance is to be attained. Management must seek an understanding of the sentiments, attitudes, and expectations of employees.

WHAT DO EMPLOYEES WANT?

What are some of the basic sentiments of employees? All of us are taught as children that we should learn to stand on our feet, become independent, and do things for ourselves. Centralized authority in business runs contrary to this basic belief. Power in industry normally passes from the top down. As a rule employees are not asked for their opinion. They are told what to do. But workers do want to have some share in determining some of the conditions and arrangements under which they work and to contribute something of their own to the way they perform the job. Supervisors and managers who understand this basic sentiment will use their authority and discretion in accordance with the expectations of their subordinates.

Americans respect the square-shooter and want a fair deal. They expect fair treatment and they resent favoritism. Violation of the rules of the game can easily upset employee morale.

In the industrial setting, progress and opportunity mean that employees look for the opportunity to advance. A man who works for a company for many years feels he has the right to more recognition and increased security. The average employee wants to get ahead.

In addition to such values as independence, fairness, and opportunity, employees also possess certain attitudes regarding their own status and the status of others with whom they work. An employee's status determines and is determined by how he feels toward the people with whom he comes in contact. The worker, like each of us, possesses a self-image. His job activities and work associations must support this self-image if he is to derive satisfaction from his work environment. Every phase of his activity symbolizes and reflects the role the employee occupies in the social system of the factory. Thus a member of a maintenance crew acts and feels differently from a lathe operator. In every instance the individual employee adjusts his behavior to his place in the organization, to the special requirements and physical surroundings of the job, and to the sentiments and habits of the group to which he belongs.

Each worker develops patterns of friendships and reactions to various informal leaders. He becomes a member of a clique. These patterns of relationship cannot be controlled by the formal organization of the company or by the intentions of management.

It is this informal social organization of one's friends and associates and the accompanying sentiments which set standards of behavior and determine the amount and kind of work which will be performed. In this area of informal relations the employee finds basic social satisfaction. An employee's morale is compounded of his feelings toward others around him and his perceptions of how they feel toward him. These feelings are a significant part of one's conception of oneself. If the employee feels psychologically effective, he is likely to be more productive.

SUPERIORS AND SUBORDINATES

Americans share the basic idea that all men are equal. However sound this may be politically, it is not true in many areas. Parents are not equal to children, nor older brothers to younger sisters. There are different social and economic classes, differentials in intellectual, professional, and social status.

This is especially true in industry where a chain of command leads from the top of the organization to the bottom. There is a hierarchy of authority, a system of superiors giving orders to subordinates.

Every person within an industrial organization, with the possible exception of the president (and the president is responsible to a board of directors), has a superior. To the employee his immediate superior is the most important person in the industry. His superior is the link with his future in the organization. Thus every subordinate is concerned with how his superior feels about him. The employee wonders if his work is satisfactory to his superior, if he makes a good appearance, if he is fulfilling the expectations his superior has regarding his work. He wants to feel important and respected.

Every superior in turn feels this way about his superior. The obverse is also true. Superiors generally are not much concerned with how their subordinates feel about them. They do not worry about the opinions of their subordinates. The superior is judging his subordinates in the light of what *his* superior would think about the people for whom he is responsible. The supervisory structure is a status system. Each level of supervision has higher status and prestige than the ones below it.

THE STATUS OF WORKERS

The matters of relative status, of where each employee fits in terms of it, and how employees compare themselves with each other, present the most irritating problems of people at work. Their resolution constitutes the problem of employee morale and increased production.

Let us glance at some of the distinctions which characterize one's status and position in industry. An obvious distinction is that between the shop and white collar jobs. Office jobs are supposed in some sense to be superior to shop jobs; the work of the office is of higher importance than the work of the operator on the line. The shop operators, the office workers think, have dirty hands, smelly clothes, are loud-mouthed and less intellectual.

Executives have something of the same attitudes toward subordinate supervisors, the skilled workers toward the semi-skilled. Every one in a factory looks down on someone, or looks up to someone, and is continuously contrasting and comparing himself with what others think or might say about him.

The rate of pay is another basis for status distinction. In industry one's importance is evaluated in terms of money return. The higher the pay, the higher the status. A $20,000 a year salesman is superior to an $.85 per hour maintenance man. A $1.80 an hour skilled operator is superior to an $.85 an hour stock boy. An employee came to see me one day threatening to resign. I was then in the personnel department of a large organization. He complained that a fellow employee doing the same job was receiving more money than he was and since they were both employed at the same time, he felt this was unfair. He was receiving $1.80 an hour and his fellow worker $1.81 an hour. I asked him whether he would make the same complaint if he were making $2.00 an hour and his fellow employee $2.01 an hour. He replied, "Certainly, he is no better than I am." It wasn't the penny differential which was bothering him. It was his feeling of importance. He had to feel he was just as important as his fellow worker.

Seniority is also a basis for status difference. Older employees feel superior to younger people or newcomers and expect more deference and greater privileges.

SYMBOLS OF STATUS

Every employee is concerned about his status. Status is indicated by the kind of clothes one is expected to wear, the desk or bench one works at, the position of the desk, the kind of machine one operates, the washroom one uses, whether one shares a locker or has a separate compartment, where and when one eats, how much time one has for lunch, whether or not one is listed in the company's telephone directory, whether there is a name plate on the desk, what floor one works on, whether one punches time or does not, whether one is paid by the hour or by the week, the kind of parking space reserved for one.

Symbols of status are a major concern, and sudden, unexplained shifts in them cause a disturbance. The employee feels insecure and threatened because his status is uncertain.

MEETING CHANGE

Other important changes also seriously affect employee morale.

Almost every one of us is upset when we are called upon to adjust to marked changes in ourselves or in our environment. We are upset because we are not prepared for the changes. They come suddenly. If we are gradually prepared, the shock is spent. We have time to consider what is likely to happen, to explore alternatives, and to get used to new expectations and consequences.

Small groups of employees who work together develop common interests. They learn what to expect from each other and what is expected from them. They learn their jobs, the peculiarities of the supervisor, the habits of the fellow workers. Knowing what to expect and to anticipate, they are psychologically comfortable. The job runs smoothly and satisfactory personal relations are worked out. Common goals and the means of achieving them are informally agreed upon. One's status is clear and one's position definite. In brief, a working social system is established. Any significant and unusual change suddenly introduced disturbs the established balance and tends toward disorder. The change may be one of personnel, management, technology, physical place of work, rules, layoff, and change in shifts.

An illustration or two will make this clear. How does an employee feel when he is suddenly shifted from one job to another without prior notice? What happens when an employee finds himself working with new fellow employees? What happens if several of your fellow workers no longer report for work, and there is no explanation? Again, how does an employee feel if a known and friendy supervisor is suddenly removed and a strange foreman starts doing things in a different way, and makes different and unaccustomed demands? How does an employee feel if some of his tools are removed without any explanation or a new machine is taken away and an old one substituted without any notice to him? What happens if arrangements are suddenly shifted or new safety devices are introduced without prior notice? How does an employee feel about getting a 24-hour notice of a lay-off? Do not these sudden changes disturb one's feeling of security?

Whenever possible, everyone should have a chance to share in a decision regarding changes which affect him. The employee should be encouraged to participate in the change to be brought about before it is introduced. The gradual introduction of change enables the worker to get used to the new arrangements. He then has the feeling that he is not being pushed around and is not being used. He gets the feeling that whatever takes place is the result, in part, of his own decision. Even in a situation where changes have to be made regardless of the view of the worker an explanation before the change is made will help. The demoralizing effects of sudden change are thus minimized.

PROBLEMS IN COMMUNICATION

The informal structure of industry is more important than the formal. The neatly arranged formal chart of the organization is far removed from the realities of the company's practices. *People* apply rules and administer directives. The rules do not apply themselves. How policies will be applied depends upon the intelligence, understanding, sensitivity, and skills of the subordinates responsible for administering them.

Officials, managers, superintendents, general foreman, supervisors, are all accustomed to the privileges and prerequisites of their office and status. Subordinates and superiors expect certain behavior in relation to each other while carrying out their respective functions and responsibilities. Traditionally, these expectations are supported by titles, salary differentials or wages, office space, proper dress, parking privileges, and eating facilities.

The awareness of one's status and role and the accompanying prestige and esteem inflate the ego. It makes one feel important especially if the person senses his inadequacy. An individual who possesses relatively little control over himself is driven to exercise control over others. He needs to control others to reassure himself that he does count. Not having learned to fight *with* his own conflicts and their accompanying (and often unconscious) tensions, he must fight *against* others and bend them to his will.

Anyone who carefully observes the day to day relations between subordinates and superiors or who is aware of what is left out of reports is struck by the double talk and half-written reports. *Communication is bottlenecked by fear of disapproval of a superior.* The subordinate generally informs his superior about matters which will indicate that things are running smoothly and denies, distorts, or omits from the account anything which would appear to be unfavorable. The important thing is to appear in good light so that one's own position is solidified and improved.

One gets ahead generally by demonstrating the good points of one's performance, not by pointing out his failures or that of his superiors. You respond to the questions of your superior according to what you think he wants to hear not to what you judge he should know.

Suppose the superior felt free and comfortable and unthreatened by his subordinate. Suppose the subordinate were convinced that the superior wanted the real facts in every case in order to improve conditions or to remove inequities. Suppose he trusted the superior and knew the latter would forthrightly communicate up the line and make an honest effort to resolve the problem presented. Would not the subordinate then be encouraged to communicate? Who of us does not long for the chance to talk straight, to say what we mean and express how we feel, assured of understanding without reproach or disagreement without retaliation?

The superior is unlikely to generate and communicate such atmosphere unless *his* superior helps him to feel free in communication. This holds true up to top levels of management.

Communication generally is characterized by having to prove oneself in the right and the other in the wrong. We don't easily listen to others, trying to understand them. We wait (not always) for the other to finish what he is saying so that we can start our defense or attack. Defensiveness isn't always obvious to the person unskilled in the process of communication. There can be a great deal of polite palaver, "I see what you mean but ——— hocus pocus."

The frustration of many sensitive, earnest, and competent personnel managers is obvious to anyone intimately acquainted with this area. A point is reached where the personnel manager is prepared to undertake a promising development program. His proposals to his superior are pigeonholed, not given a fair hearing, or simply ignored. In so many cases, the personnel manager complains that the superiors do not want what is proposed because they do not believe in genuine communication.

A telling illustration reached me in a letter from the personnel manager of one of America's large industrial organizations.

Off the record, I have analyzed my situation many times and I say over and over again, I must have a lot of first cousins within industry whose real objectives are being smothered for lack of personnel oxygen of his boss.

It has been a very slow process trying to introduce a few of the many principles we should be using today to help our supervisory organization and our people. I am talking about 600 supervisors of several levels and 8000 people who report to them. I simply cannot get my program started since no one in a responsible position wants to support it. They simply talk a good game.

I do not give up without a real struggle when I know that the personnel principles you and I and many others support are basically sound. But, there is a limit to one's physical and emotional endurance, and I regret to report that I am beginning to submit rather than widen the breach. It's grand to be able to write to you and unload some of this.

Industrial managers complain about the failure of communication, not realizing that often they are the blocks. They have reached the top. They are the important people. They possess the know-how, the power, and the authority. Why don't their subordinates listen to them? They want morale improved—but without changes in policy and processes.

Communication is a two-way process. Why do not superiors listen, hear, and understand what is being said to them? One reason is, little of importance is being said. Why? Because subordinates are expected to listen. They have not been encouraged to exercise discretion, to make mistakes without being penalized, to disagree without feeling guilty and insecure. If we really tried to understand another, our own view would have to be modified or changed. We would then experience confusion or annoyance. We do not want to make the effort to reorganize our thinking and feeling. Self-criticism is never comfortable.

Good communication is a function of fine morale. If a staff or line manager is responsible for given policies or procedure he must also be given the discretion to administer them in his own way. He may have his own solution to a problem but he is willing to permit his subordinates to resolve it in their own way. He encourages participation and does not penalize difference of opinion. The sensitive leader does not insist on the rigid application of rules or carrying out a given policy to the letter. Rules are rules but people are people. The rules are made to help the organization, not to be enforced because they are the rules.

Good communication depends upon good morale. Respecting subordinates, encouraging and accepting differences of opinion, easily admitting one's misjudgments and mistakes, exploring situations rather than condemning the people involved, encouraging experimentation not followed by an "I told you so," relating to people for whom you are responsible and to whom you report in a friendly, accepting atmosphere, demonstrating one's capacity to continue to learn from subordinates,—these are some of the qualities of leadership which create the kind of morale out of which genuine communication arises.

The size and complexity of large-scale industry create inevitable difficulties in communication. This fact of structure is an impersonal matter for which no one can be held personally responsible. After overall policy is planned and regulations set up the administration should be delegated to the various levels of authority. Every manager should know the extent of his authority and responsibility. His superior can communicate to him that within *that* area the manager is free and is expected to administer *and interpret* company policy and rule.

There are two advantages. The manager acquires a real sense of participation in company practice. He is making a creative contribution and feels himself an important part of the organization. His superior depends upon *him*. Furthermore, in stating that the manager is expected *to interpret* policies and rules rather than to apply them mechanically, the superior is expressing directly what occurs in any case. Top management does not then have to wonder why and where communication has broken down. When discretion is given, responsibility can be located.

Communication can be improved when the people engaged in a specific task feel that others have confidence in their ability, trust their judgment, and want their help. Subordinates cannot feel this way unless superiors share this feeling. Communication up the line increases in proportion to the humility communicated down the line.

AUTHORITY AND DEMOCRACY IN INDUSTRY

An industrial organization is not a clinic for employees' personal problems. A primary and legitimate objective of private industry is to manufacture and sell goods or services for a profit.

But employees are people and the way they feel about the job and toward the people with whom they work must be taken into account as an important factor in the production of goods.

Management generally believes that its concern is to define policy, issue directives, and, through the formal organization of divided responsibility on the part of its line and staff managers, have its orders carried out. Management possesses the authority, and often finds it difficult to share authority or to qualify its exercise.

Obviously, industry cannot operate without authority resting somewhere. There must be submission to authority because it is either desirable or inevitable. Authority can neither arise nor be preserved without establishing and maintaining distance between those who command and those who obey.

Does authority with its accompanying fears of status distinctions and social distance prevent genuine communication between superiors and subordinates? The answer depends upon one's conception of authority, which can be viewed as the ruthless exercise of one's power and position or as resting on an ethical foundation, a sense of obligation to others.

The manager who possesses an awareness of what people are like and what happens during their association is more likely to consider the feelings, sentiments, and attitudes of employees as well as the logic of policy, procedure, and production. He will develop insight into what employees expect from their jobs, from their superiors, and fellow workers. He will develop a wide appreciation of the problems of communication, of change, of the importance of status and sentiments. If he pursues these paths he will gradually recognize that sooner or later he must face the dilemma of profits *versus* people. In a showdown, which is more important, producing goods or respecting the dignity of people?

Fortunately the dilemma is not as sharp in practice as it is in the statement of it. In day to day activities many superiors and subordinates can and do relate to each other in a friendly, understanding way. The quality of these relationships will reflect the superior's understanding of the social and psychological needs of employees.

In the long run, genuine respect for, and interest in the employee as a person, results in increased production. More sensitive awareness of the fact that an industrial setting is not merely a place where so many hands work for a wage, but a place where human beings spend their days fulfilling their needs as social beings will result in increased satisfaction both for managers and employees.[1]

NOTES

1. For those who wish to read further on industry as a social system, consult:

W. F. Whyte, *Human Relations in the Restaurant Industry* (New York: McGraw-Hill, 1948).

Daniel Katz and H. Hyman, "Morale in War Industries," in Hartley and Newcomb (eds.), *Readings in Social Psychology* (New York: Henry Holt, 1947) p. 437, 447.

George Homans, "Group Factors in Worker Productivity," Hartley and Newcomb, *op. cit.*, p. 448-460.

Wilbert E. Moore, *Industrial Relations and the Social Order* (New York: Macmillan, 1946).

Industry and Society, edited by William F. Whyte (New York: McGraw-Hill, 1946), contains the views of eight outstanding leaders.

Chris Argyris, "Human Relations in a Bank," *Harvard Business Review*, Vol. 32, 1954, p. 63-72.

Chris Argyris, *Diagnosing Human Relations in Organizations, A Case Study of a Hospital* (New Haven: Yale University Press, 1956).

III

THE FUNCTION OF A MANAGER

THE main purpose of an industrial enterprise is to manufacture, distribute, or sell economic services or goods.
Management's job is to carry out this purpose. Raw materials,
capital investment, technical knowledge, and consumer need
all enter as necessary factors in carrying on a successful business. The most important resource, however, is the human
one. Man's creativity results in an output that cannot be
measured by input. To be sure, the performance of able
managers will be reflected in increased production or more
effective services, but no one has yet succeeded in quantifying
the spirit of performance, the will to work, the satisfaction of
achievement, the respect of one's peers.

The manager's function is to assist others to develop themselves in carrying out their assigned tasks in the organization.
Both the manager and the people who are directly associated
with him in the organization must keep clearly in mind what
their respective limits of operation and responsibility are.

The manager is not responsible for carrying out the duties
of his assistants. The assistant to the manager does not assist
the manager in *his* job. He carries on his own job, namely, that
assigned to an assistant manager. The manager *is* responsible

for helping the assistant to discover how he can perform his own objectives more effectively and how to make the best use of his potentialities to carry out his, the subordinate's, assigned responsibilities.

The manager helps his associates only with regard to the objectives of the company which control, define, and limit the activities of both the manager and his associates. There is a formal structure of the industry or business within which all who are connected with the industry or business must operate. Certain rules of procedure and lines of authority give direction to the enterprise. There are certain moral, ethical, and legal assumptions underlying the operation of the industry which often remain unexpressed.

A clear recognition on the part of managers of the limits of their responsibility toward fellow workers and the power and authority structure within which they operate would lessen frustration and reduce tension between the several levels of management as well as the members of any one department.

To illustrate the limited function of a manager I shall present excerpts from several workshops attended by personnel managers. I shall show that the manager who tries to help his associates without recognizing that it is *job performance which sets the limits* to the kind of help he can offer gets confused and does not perform effectively. By making more explicit the power and authority structure of industry, managers are in a better position to understand the nature and extent of their own authority and power, the limits within which they can assist their subordinates. A recognition that *industry is management-centered* will clarify the limits within which managers can function and will protect their own integrity. They will not try to function in ways which the structure of their organization prevents. Finally, I shall try to show how managers working together may play a part in determining the direction of company objectives, in restructuring rules of procedure, and even in modifying basic, implicit assumptions.[1]

INDIVIDUAL NEEDS AND JOB PERFORMANCE

Sometimes the function of personnel administration departments or divisions is carried by the director of personnel or a training director, who in some organizations is the chief of a department and, in others, reports to the director of personnel. The term "function" is inaccurate since in the majority of organizations such departments are multifunctional.[2]

Most of the work of personnel managers has little to do directly with persons. It is concerned chiefly with clerical and administrative duties such as employee ratings, pension plans, wage rates, safety, job evaluation, and job analysis. These functions are important but at the same time account for the hollowness of the work of personnel departments.

Personnel managers should be concerned with persons. Ideally, perhaps, there should not be any personnel department. Every manager is a personnel manager whatever his department happens to be. His important function is to encourage those who work with him to perform well, and better, *the job* for which they are responsible.

This does not mean that the employee's or subordinate's needs are to be ignored. It does mean that only certain needs are relevant, those which bear on his work for the organization. The preceding remarks do not exclude attention to the human being as a person. In fact, the highest regard for the person is evidenced in trying to be of help only in the area for which one is responsible and for which one possesses special competence. The manager represents the company and has special competence in a limited area. This limit defines the area of operation. The manager's job is to assist the employee in well-defined, limited areas. The employee uses that help to accomplish his assigned job. Both share responsibility for their respective assignments and together move forward in carrying out the purposes of the organization. Otherwise why are they working together for the particular organization on a specific problem in a specific setting?

As employees' needs and problems in or out of the plant *affect job performance* they become relevant. This statement can be driven to an absurd point. One can argue that no act of any person is unrelated to any other act of his. Logically and psychologically this is sound enough.[3] An individual, however, is not helped generally but always in some specific context. Needs are met and problems are solved not in a vacuum but in contact with specific situations. What happens by way of resolution of the *specific* difficulty *may* have far-reaching effects in other areas. This, however, is beyond the control of anyone except the individual involved.

The manager and employee are human beings with many kinds of needs and problems. This must never be lost sight of. But management cannot effectively be concerned with all of the persons at work. This will not help the people or the industry. The people who are *employed* must be engaged in resolving the problems which arise *there* within the limits defined by the overall purposes of the organization and the specific tasks assigned to them.

Human behavior is a complicated affair. It is not always easy for a manager to decide which problems of an employee are directly relevant to job performance. Every employee brings himself to the job; it is a *person* who works. His wants and needs as a person cannot easily be separated from his wants and needs as an employee. This fact gives point to the need of trying to distinguish between them. An awareness of the need to focus on job performance, to appreciate the need for limits, will help the manager to make sounder judgments than he would otherwise make regarding the kind of help he extends and under what circumstances he extends it.[4]

The following exchange is a telling illustration of this. We had been discussing the importance of focusing on one's job and the need for well-defined limits:

GORDON: I find it hard to understand this need for limits.

TED: This business of focus has me all mixed up. What I get out of it so far is that I've been doing too many things.

DOUG: That certainly is true in my job. I can see what is happening to me. My title is Coordinator of Personnel Research. I can see now what has been frustrating me. I have hundreds of different activities and I don't know from one minute to the next what I'm doing. What I need is a coordinator. (Laughter.)

TED: Or else a clear idea of focus. (Laughter.)

CHARLES: At a meeting last week our personnel manager wanted to know why he was responsible for having windows cleaned in our factory. The discussion got pretty hot. Everyone was angry. I can see now what the problem was.

LEADER: Namely. . . .

CHARLES: Well, it's simple, now. He was trying to find out just what his focus was as a personnel manager.

LEADER: It seems we can appreciate at this point that without a specific structure within which any manager or supervisor operates, that is, without a focus which limits what one does, you cannot do a good job. Sound organization is a prerequisite for freedom of activity. If there are no limits, aimlessness results. No one knows what to expect or what is required or who is responsible for what.

I could have made this statement much earlier in the discussion. Most of the participants would not have understood the point if made earlier. The discussion immediately following my statement indicates the group was ready to discuss the implications of limits and focus:

TED: Gee, I'm beginning to see something. I've been bothered the whole past year by something which I'm just beginning to understand. As personnel manager of our plant I'm supposed to help people. But no one has ever defined for me what's meant by "helping people." The supervisors come to me and I'm supposed to help them but I've never known the kind of help I'm supposed to give.

Let me give you one example. We had a supervisor with a great deal of friction in his home over finances. He came to see me. I'm ashamed to tell you that I set up a set of books for him and his wife and told him how to budget his take-home pay. In fact, and I feel foolish now, I distributed his salary from time to time, told his wife what to buy, how much to deposit in the bank. When I get back to my job next week I'm going to give him his bank book and tell him to settle his own problems. That's certainly none of *my* business.

GORDON: O.K., but don't you think, Ted, there are situations where a supervisor has the right to depend on you?

ARTHUR: May I give an example of that? Suppose a supervisor comes in and tells you that an employee, So and So, is no good. What are you going to do about it? Is that the kind of situation you mean, Gordon?

GORDON: Yes, that would be one kind.

ARTHUR: I think the training director should say in a quiet way, "I think that is your job, it's up to you." I've been guilty many times of doing what Ted does.

TED: It isn't easy to tell others, "That's your job, and I can't be of help to you."

LEADER: Why isn't it easy, Ted?

TED: Oh, I get it. It would be easy if you knew exactly what your job was, your limits. Then you wouldn't have to feel badly. You're doing your job.

ARTHUR: And a lot depends on the way you say it. If you're sure of what you're doing, you'll express yourself quietly.

TED: I think the worst feature of what I have been doing is robbing the other person of a chance to assume responsibility.

ARTHUR: I can see now that wanting to be kind and considerate to employees can sometimes be simply sticky sentimentality that is a trap unless you understand what you are doing. I mean, your function.

CHARLES: This all adds up to what we've been calling "being professional." You can be friendly and firm. If an employee or supervisor asked the training director to help him and the help he asked for is no part of the training director's job the training director takes the attitude, "I'm sorry. That's not my responsibility. You have your job and I have mine."

TED: I'd like to put it this way. Don't carry another person's load, but help the person carry his own load, *if* that is part of your job.

BERT: Art and I were discussing this last night. We had been told time and again by our executive vice-president that supervisors are supposed to know all about their employees. That seems to me now to be ridiculous and impossible. The vice-president must have read an article in one of the personnel journals. (Laughter.) The supervisor is working for a corporation and he doesn't have to know the private business or family life of his employees.

LEADER: Are you saying that a supervisor should not comment to the employee on some bit of news he has learned about the supervisor's family or his out-of-plant activity?

BERT: I'm not saying that. He can be friendly without being an inquisitive busybody.

BILL: By the same token, then, Ted should not say to the employee, "Here is your bank book, that's your problem." He might, without going out of line, tell him where he could obtain help in learning how to budget. Ted could tell him that he and the other employees, all of us, contribute to the Community Chest and he is entitled to that kind of service of the Family Society if he wants help.

TED: Then suppose he says he would like help. Am I in order calling up the agency for him? Is that part of my responsibility?

BOB: In light of our discussion I would say no. I think if you told him the name of the agency it would be up to him to make the contact and you could wish him luck.

TED: Suppose there is no service of that kind for employees and there are no social agencies in the small town. Now what does the supervisor say or do?

BOB: If a guy is down and needs help we had better be sure that any help we give is in accord with our responsibility as a training director or personnel manager. (A rather long silence.)

LEADER: I wonder if Ted's question was answered?

Here, I was trying to raise the question regarding the difficulties of becoming too rigid in holding to one's limits and focus:

BOB: We seem to agree that supervisors have no responsibility for the personal problems of employees.

LEADER: Unless they directly affect his work.

Bob: If they do, we should help.

Ted: If we had no agencies in our community should *I* budget for my supervisor?

Bob: I would say no. Budgeting his family expenses has little to do with the job he is doing for the company. If he worried about his children not studying piano, I don't think *you* would want to provide a music teacher or the money for the lessons. At least not in your capacity as personnel manager. What you do as an individual is your own business.

Leader: Then what happens to the supervisor who has trouble in budgeting?

Bob: I don't know. What happens to any of us with problems having nothing to do with our job? We try and do what we can with the help of friends or loan agencies or whatnot.

MANAGEMENT-CENTERED INDUSTRY

Bob's last remarks express simply and directly the inescapable presence of a world of people, objects, time, and circumstances in which and with which every individual must come to grips. There are given realities over which we have little, if any, control. A person who decides upon employment in an organization is bound to accept the conditions, rules, and regulations under which that organization operates. The conditions, rules, and regulations may be modified for one reason or another. There is no escaping from the fact, however, that some organization or structure must be present. Without limits choice becomes impossible. Every manager and employee of the organization will soon run into associates or situations which present difficulties. If the individual had the choice, matters (limits) could be arranged differently. But the individual's choice is limited by the inherent need of organized regulations for an ongoing company.

Besides the objective need for rules and regulations there is another limitation on individual need or preference. The rules and regulations are administered with regard to the specific objective of the organization which is, generally, to operate as a successful enterprise.

The field of human relations, especially human relations in industry, has received intensive attention during the past twenty years. Higher management recognizes that employee morale needs to be improved and that management training or management development is necessary for more effective performance. The attention to and recognition of such needs cannot be too highly praised. The danger is growing that these movements may become formal rituals. A careful reading of the growing literature and a rigorous analysis of the actual practices support this opinion.[5]

The relationship between employee satisfaction and increased production is not as simple or as direct as has been assumed. Productivity, for example, may be merely the means to other employee goals rather than the result of worker satisfaction. Workers who are dissatisfied with their jobs may, because of a threat of loss of the job, produce at a very high rate.[6]

Human motivation is rarely directed solely by economic considerations. Innumerable studies of employee attitudes in heavy industry, the retail trades, and utility corporations have conclusively shown this. Average employees, along with professional workers, seek a large number of noneconomic goals which stem from the social values of the classes to which they belong. Many workers are not motivated toward social achievement. They do not particularly care to "get ahead."

They belong to a segment of society where the middle-class or higher middle-class values are simply not operating in their lives. The assumption that all workers want to improve their social status may be a projection of the bias of the middle-class investigators.[7]

The problem of higher productivity and employee morale is also complicated by the relations of the employee to his union. Getting ahead in the union hierarchy may not depend upon increased output for the company. Social status and advancement in the union organization may be negatively correlated with increased production.

What of the relation between increased output and quality of product? If speed is at a premium the quality of the product may suffer. If high quality work is desired, the rate of production is lowered. Employee satisfaction follows from performing a job meaningfully and skillfully. This takes more time than performing a routine job quickly but without much satisfaction in exercising one's creative ability.

Some studies have shown that dissatisfied workers, those who are critical of company policy, are the highest producers. One investigator reports that a year after all workers in the factory had filled out a questionnaire those who had been promoted to foremen positions had been more dissatisfied with company practices than those who were not promoted.[8]

The relationships between employee attitudes and employee performance are not sufficiently clear to justify the assumption that setting up a program of human relations will *ipso facto* increase production. A training program for supervisors or a management development program for executives in this area is merely a piece of machinery. The assumptions and objectives require careful analyses before their soundness is established. Without such careful examination of what these programs rest upon their unquestioned acceptance is likely to become a new fad.

The foregoing discussion of human relations was introduced in the context of management-centered industry to reveal the limits of a manager's responsibility. Superficially the widespread acceptance of the need for training in this area, and the need for helping management to understand it, would seem to contradict the fact that employees have to accept narrower limits than a quarter of a century ago. In a sense this is so. There is increased recognition on the part of management that the cooperation and participation of employees will improve good will, strengthen loyalty, and lead to friendly adjustment of differences between management and union. The day of hard-fisted, autocratic exercise of unilateral authority on the part of corporations is fast disappearing. This change has come about not only through labor's coming of age but also from better insight into the psychological and sociological factors leading to better production.

Management today seeks control preponderantly through persuasion rather than through naked power. *Genuine* cooperative participation, that is, the *actual* sharing of policy and decision making, on the part of management and unions, so that the business is conducted on a joint rather than a unilateral basis, is extremely rare. The ready acceptance of the need for human relations training and for executive development in that area, in the absence of sound knowledge of the relations between employee satisfaction and increased production, may mean that management is using the language, symbols and devices to create a pseudo-democratic atmosphere in which control of management's policy is exercised more smoothly. This may not be deliberate deception and pretense as much as self-deception on the part of management.

The unwitting use of democratic procedures and symbols to disguise benevolent despotism is a stock in trade of parents and of leaders in business, government, and education. The "progressive," democratic upper-middle-class mother who sweetly inquires of her teen-age daughter, "Mary, would you like to help with the dishes?" would probably change her tune—or tone—if Mary surprisingly rejoined, "You mean I really have a choice?"

The spirit of cooperation between management and employees is not being underestimated. There are many areas and issues in which employers and employees genuinely cooperate. A great deal of arbitrary control, direction through deceptive persuasion, and sincere democratic procedure exists in the same organization depending on the importance of the issue. Basically, however, *the ultimate authority and power reside in management. Industry is management-centered.* This is the reality in which employees find themselves. No amount of talk and no number of democratic devices can conceal this fact.[9]

There are also basic power structures in education, unions, government, religious, and political organizations. I am not making any moral judgment. I am trying to describe the true context in which managers carry out their responsibility of helping others to develop. Within the limitations described it is still possible for management and employees to accomplish a great deal for each other. More could be accomplished if both management and labor were on an equal footing regarding power to decide on production schedules, job evaluation, promotion, planning, plant expansion, pricing, and other basic policies.[10]

Let us restate the principal issue being discussed. A manager should be aware of the framework within which he is operating. He should not be deceived nor should he deceive himself or others. He should be clear about the structure and assumptions under which he is working. Through understanding the limits within which he carries out his duties, he realizes what he can do and what he may not do. This minimizes dissatisfactions, frustrations, and dilemmas. If he realizes the nature of the framework in which he operates, he is free to make a choice of working within it responsibly and loyally, of resigning, or of remaining and trying legitimately to change the rules and regulations. If he makes the first or third choice, he will not be split in carrying on his duties *if he is aware* of the limits he accepts.

Satisfying human relations in any area are inherently desirable. Employee good will, friendly union-management relations, and regard for the dignity of the employee are effective factors in freeing creative ability. Waste and inefficiency will thereby be reduced and production increased. Research in industrial relations *tends* to show that an employee's production does increase when he receives attention from his manager, knows that he is respected as a worker, knows where he stands, has a chance for promotion, feels there is someone willing to help him, has some say in the conditions of his work, plays some role in changes which are to be introduced, knows his opinion is sought for and respected regarding his work, and knows his suggestions for improvement are welcomed.

The important matter is the attitude of the manager. If the introduction of industrial psychologists and personnel managers and employee benefits and services are paternalistic devices intended to *manipulate* workers into "cooperative" employees who will increase production, it is unlikely that the full use of the human resources in industry will be made. If, on the other hand, a manager has attained a mature, adult understanding of his own struggles in growing, of the conflicts one has to deal with and live with, and has attained a sustaining amount of self-respect, he will inevitably bear respect for others as they engage in similar struggles in the industrial setting. Inescapably the objective is a successful industrial or business enterprise as the manager works *with* others. He works with them and *wants to* help them. This he, the manager, finds eminently satisfying. He uses himself for others in the common, limited objectives of their organization. Genuine respect for employees and increased production can go together. Here is an example:

A paper company made a series of contracts with independent farmers to supply them with wood. The company's practice was to ask each of the contractors to supply more wood than would be needed in any given season. The reason for this practice was that invariably some of the contractors would either fail in making deliveries or would supply less than the share agreed upon. On the whole, the amount of wood received from all of the contractors averaged out to the requirements of the year.

Some of the contractors furnished wood to more than one

paper company. Contractor X, however, who had extensive holdings in woodlands, usually furnished all of his cut wood to the paper company in question:

TOM: (The treasurer of a division of the company.) I'd rather not listen to another telephone call like the one I heard yesterday. Pete knows what I mean.

PETE: (Who reports to Tom.) You mean the call from X. I told him off and I mean off. I hung up on him before he hung up on me.

LEADER: Pete, are you free to tell us about it?

PETE: X delivered five thousand cordage of wood last week and we refused to take delivery of more than three thousand. We have all the wood we need. I tried to explain this to X but he wouldn't listen.

JOHN: (In charge of purchasing and reporting to Pete.) X spoke to me in the morning and insisted we accept the full amount since that is what we contracted for. He invested money in having it cut and I think we should have accepted it.

PETE: We couldn't use it and besides we haven't got the storage space for it.

JOHN: Then we shouldn't have contracted for that amount of wood.

PETE: And suppose we were caught short as we were two years ago? Remember we had to pay premium prices to cover that shortage?

JOHN: I fail to see what that has to do with our obligation to X.

TOM: Even if we had storage space the company would be foolish to tie up investment in wood that cannot be used during the current year.

HENRY: I understand that X said he'd sell the whole lot to Superior Paper Company and never cut another piece of wood for us.

PETE: That's bad. But I was under instructions not to accept any more wood.

JOHN: I was under instructions from you, Pete, to contract with X for five thousand cord and I did.

TOM: I don't see what all the fuss is about. You all know our practice has been to order more than we need to be certain we'll get all that we want. The contractors know that's been our custom.

JOHN: Yes, they've known that and they haven't liked it. But they can't afford to sue on the contracts which aren't worth much anyway. You know the contracts stipulate that the amounts of wood ordered are subject to change.

PETE: Then you agree, John, we have no obligation to X?

JOHN: (Heatedly.) I most certainly do not agree. We may not be legally responsible but we led X, one of our chief suppliers, to believe that we had to have that full amount. He hired loggers and spent a great deal of money getting that wood. We should have taken it all or taken any part of it and paid him the full amount.

PETE: Well, I was acting under Tom's orders to refuse the delivery.

TOM: The central office sent out instructions not to purchase any more wood.

LEADER: I take it that the central office doesn't know about X's relation to this division?

I deliberately introduced the central office's responsibility in the matter at this point to help Tom modify his attitude which, in turn, would help Pete crystallize his own feelings:

TOM: Yes, they do.

JOHN: Then I certainly think X should be paid.

TOM: I suppose the good will would be worth it.

JOHN: It's not merely a matter of good will. We are morally bound to pay even if we're not legally responsible. X fulfilled his part and we let him down.

PETE: You know I feel like a heel hanging up on X. I think John is right.

LEADER: Maybe you thought so yesterday when you hung up on X in Tom's presence?

PETE: You mean I felt guilty because I knew X was right but at the same time I had to carry out Tom's order?

LEADER: Well, is that what you mean? (Laughter.)

PETE: That's exactly what took place. Tom, I honestly think John is right and the company policy with the contractors has to be changed. We can build extra storage space and what we lose in tying up capital we can gain in not having to pay premium prices when we are caught short on supplies.

The final outcome of the policy is not our concern. What is of interest is the altered attitudes of John, Tom, and Pete. Tom, the treasurer, Pete, the divisional manager, and John, the purchasing agent, are responsible to each other respectively. John places a moral issue ahead of narrow company interest. Pete, his manager, is willing to learn from him and does. By agreeing with Pete, he encourages Pete to speak his piece freely. Tom, their manager, is also amenable to modifying his stand. His willingness to reconsider the matter is encouraging to the other managers. *All three managers are in the process of modifying a traditional practice of this large paper company*. A moral obligation is being placed ahead of the financial gain. The important point, in this context, is that the three managers can learn from each other and probably deepen their loyalty to the company, that is, to each other as associated managers of that division.

John's integrity as a person is *directly* related to the purchasing problem in question. At the start, Pete and Tom are trying to state the limits within which they all operate. The company's policy had been laid down in previous years. John is dissatisfied with the prevailing power structure which had taken advantage of the sub-contractors. His vision, persistence, and integrity were communicated to the others and thus will probably add to the future success of the company.

The sub-contractor X (who may be considered as an employee) was not in a position of equal strength with the company. Nevertheless, the end result was satisfying to both parties. The case was cited to indicate that unilateral power can be used to avoid conflict. Common goals of management and labor can be recognized even if the opposing sides are not equal in authority or power. It is the *recognition* of managerial role and levels of authority and responsibility rather than the unequal power between opposing forces which often leads to conflict.

While cooperative relations are superior to conflict, the fact of the nature of the economic corporate reality should not be overlooked. Opposition between employees and their unions and the top management of the large corporations cannot be resolved by management development programs. More meaningful cooperation and more permanent resolution of many areas of conflict will result from collective bargaining between strong international unions and powerful corporations who approach a balance of bargaining power. This is viewing the future of the industrial scene as a whole. Through the growth of labor union strength, its relation to political parties and legislative action, the overriding authority of management will probably be modified. Both parties will gradually overcome their excesses, suspicions, and distrust.

Our present concern, however, is in improved relations between managers and employees *under present management-centered industry*. Management's authority is currently paramount. The manager should be clear about his role, his authority, and responsibility. Within his areas of competence, clearly defined and limited, he exercises his authority to help his associates or subordinates perform more competently, creatively, cooperatively in those areas reserved for them. These areas are growing wider each year and they differ in different organizations, large and small. Within such limits of any given plant democratic management-employee relations can be improved. Not the distribution of power but the denial of its exercise often causes much of the conflict and unrest in current management-employee relations.

A manager who recognizes this will reflect the following attitude. "This is what I can do to help you, company policy being what it is. The policies or rules or procedures have this range of resiliency. Is there something you can suggest or do within these limits, and can I be of help?" This is honest, clear, and direct. The employee or associated manager knows, too, where he stands and can act forthrightly within his limited jurisdiction.[11] Genuine respect and mutual cooperation are possible only if all parties honestly use the degree of power they possess for mutual benefit.

THE DETERMINATION OF OBJECTIVES

Ideally, one manager does not make decisions affecting another manager.[12] Every manager helps those working with him to define their objectives and to make their own decisions. Whoever is responsible for carrying out certain company action should be the one to make the decisions regarding that action. Every mother loves her own child. A manager who is given discretion to plan a job should be the one to decide on how to carry it through. Since it is his baby he will want to nourish it.

The specific objectives of individual managers must be consistent with the general overall objectives of the organization. The manager who exercises authority and control over the objectives in his own department must keep in mind the purposes of the enterprise as a whole. The function of a manager is to help others assume responsibility through their own development and effort. Inevitably, situations will arise where a subordinate manager's judgment will not jibe with the stated policy of higher management. Whose judgment controls? The manager cannot be given discretion to decide on specific objectives and then have that discretion removed if his decision is countermanded without becoming frustrated and even bitter. A manager's integrity must be protected even at the cost of error. Managers, too, learn through making mistakes. To be sure, the mistakes had better not occur too often or be too costly. The manager may have to be replaced or shifted to another job.

Let us turn to a concrete situation to make the point clear. Higher management in this particular organization decided that a training program for supervisors was sorely needed. Bob, the training director, was notified to provide a program:

BOB: I wish I knew what the supervisors needed.

TED M.: Don't you know what they need?

BOB: I don't think I do.

ART: I know what Bob is talking about. Management decides the supervisors ought to have training, but the supervisors don't recognize their own needs.

HERB: Isn't it sensible to offer what you, as training director, think they need? Some will be interested, some will reject what you offer, and others will never even get to the meeting unless they are ordered to come.

ART: I think if you challenge the few who want something, they will get to a point of recognizing their inadequacies and will tell others about what they are getting out of the meetings.

BILL: I think higher management has to take the responsibility of indicating what should go into training.

ART: That doesn't mean that the supervisors will accept direction.

BILL: Our managers have to produce goods. They have an idea of what supervisors ought to know about human relations. The problem is to find a balance between the needs of production and the needs of the employees and supervisors as human beings. I think if we talked over with the supervisors their performance against their qualifications for their own job, that would help them see what they need.

BOB: I certainly can't sit in my cubicle and dream up programs. I've got to know what the supervisors think they want, but many of them don't know what they need or will need. My superiors don't know what supervisors need. We have to balance what management thinks is needed and what we as training directors know is needed. We have to convince management of our point of view and have them really accept what we think is needed.

LEADER: You just said managers do have an idea that supervisors ought to know about human relations. Then you said your superiors don't know what supervisors need. Then you added you couldn't sit in your office and dream up programs. You finally indicated that as a training director you know what is needed. I'm not clear what your position really is.

BOB: We have to allow the supervisors to evaluate their own performance with our help so that they see what they lack. If supervisors are going to advance they have got to improve in areas where they are weak. In our own company we have frequent individual conferences with our supervisors to try to help them see how they can improve.

TED B.: You educate when the supervisors want something.

BOB: What things would supervisors need?

TED M.: Can't you name what they need?

TED B.: You can find out.

ART: That is what supervisors resent. Someone tells them what they need.

HERB: We find out what they need from listening to them. You offer them what they say they want help in if it is relevant to our work.

ART: Maybe you change them so they feel inadequate and in that way want something?

TED M.: I think through an individual rating with you, the supervisor discovers what he lacks and needs to improve.

BILL: I think management also has some right to indicate what it wants.

ART: True enough, but that's no guarantee that management will get results.

BILL: In our company we make an annual inventory of all performance. Our people are eager for training if they can see how it can benefit them. I am right in the middle of this evaluation inventory and I know that it works.

TED M.: If management supplies a training program they will all come along six months after it starts and say, "Give me a fifteen minute summary of what you are doing in training."

LEADER: Can we say that the training director has the responsibility for developing the program, that top management must support and want a program, but that the specific structuring of its contents must include what the supervisors indicate they want?

ART: Management feels that everyone *must* develop. I don't think that's always possible. Sometimes people don't want to be developed.

DON: There are a great many natural limitations in ability and interest.

ART: True, not every foreman is necessarily a potential plant manager.

LEADER: Isn't there a danger of using this as a defense against our lack of skill in helping people to develop?

ART: That's right. One should never stop trying.

LEADER: Bob asked a question and it has not been answered. How do you help people to become interested?

TED B.: I think Ted M. answered when he said we should try to help the supervisor to see what his own limitations are, what holds him back from advancement.

LEADER: You are assuming that he is interested, but what happens if he is not motivated and has no interest?

TED B.: Well, you should have enough foresight to know whose throat you can jam this down.

LEADER: I beg your pardon! (Laughter.)

TED B.: Seriously, I think you should try to present the material in such a way that you help the supervisor see what there is that he can use.

DON: The supervisor must see for himself what there is in it for him. He has got to feel that he will benefit from attending the meetings. If he doesn't see that, I don't think a training director can do anything about it.

BOB: I think we can sum this up by saying that the leader must so challenge the supervisor that he will want to participate. We should not overlook another important point. The training director must present the program to higher management levels for their genuine support.

ART: I agree. I think it is a mistake for directors to plan training programs. The emphasis must come from top management.

BOB: That is what I have been saying. We have no right to dream up programs. It is ineffective. Line management rather than the staff man has to support a program. If it doesn't come from line management the chances are they will give only lip service to any supervisory program.

GORDON: But the training directors have some responsibility in helping our own superiors in understanding this. It seems to me there are occasions when we have lunch with them or in casual conversation or in formal conference we can clarify the issues with top management. We don't have to tell them what we have in mind, but we can help them to see some of our problems and their problems. The building of the program is our responsibility. This is a long-term matter and isn't done in a day.

HERB: (An executive vice-president.) It seems to me our own management realizes people need help. Our mistake has been that our training department has used canned material. Our people come to the meetings but the programs fall flat. The trouble here isn't that management doesn't understand the need for developing supervisors. Our difficulty has been and is that we haven't got skilled leaders. The training directors don't accept their responsibility for building programs.

BOB: Your management realizes people need help. Do the people, the supervisors realize that they need help and do *they* want it? That's the important problem, isn't it? And it's the job of your training director to find out.

LEADER: Herb, who suggested the canned material?

HERB: The personnel director. He was under orders to get a program started right away.

LEADER: And he instructed the training director to obtain the canned material?

HERB: That's right.

LEADER: Is it? (Laughter.)

This excerpt shows the diffuse, loose, and confused thinking which results from a lack of clarity of objectives and responsibilities. Higher management decides that a training program for supervisors is necessary. In the first place, whoever is in charge of training should have been consulted before the decision was made. This is not to state that the *final* decision was not properly made by higher management. The propriety of such decision depends upon the allocation of duties and responsibilities in any given organization. In any case, however, since the training staff would be directly involved its representative should have been consulted.

Again, higher management undermines the personnel and training staffs by telling them to start right away. The personnel director, similarly, removes responsibility from the training director by instructing him regarding the material to be used. Bob, a training director, comes closest to realizing that it is up to the training director to help the supervisors decide what, if anything, they might desire by way of help in their problems. The general objective is a supervisory training program. This objective should be communicated to the personnel department. In turn, the personnel director communicates this to the relevant staff associate whose responsibility it is to administer such program if and when he finally decides it is in order. Each one in the management hierarchy should be left alone to carry forward his responsibilities in the manner he decides. Carrying his responsibilities includes his obligation to communicate upward as well as downward on the progress being made. In a properly organized enterprise, every manager is prepared to share whatever skill and knowledge he commands with his immediate associates when called upon to do so. The respective managers continue their learning through trying to help others carry out their responsibilities.

Here is a final excerpt which occurred toward the close of a workshop:

LEADER: What is the function of the manager of a group?

BOB: To help the members understand themselves by creating the most favorable atmosphere in which to learn.

TED B.: It's like a coxswain who directs a race but doesn't himself row. He times and structures the strokes.

CHARLES: Suppose the problem of the group is to cut down absenteeism or to conduct a meeting to discuss the absentee rate.

HERB: The leader or a member can say, "We are losing so many hours. What suggestions have you to cut down this rate?"

LEADER: Are you saying, Herb, that management expects the absentee rate to be cut down?

CHARLES: Yes, let's take that issue.

DON: Suppose the members refuse to discuss the question? They don't participate.

LEADER: What would you as the manager-leader do in a case like that?

ART: I would say, "This is our problem. What can we do about it? This is our job." I think this would be my way of challenging the group.

DOUG: Suppose your boss says, "I want the absentee rate cut down," and you say to him, "Yes, we are going to talk that over at tomorrow's meeting."

TED M.: And the boss says to me, "O.K., I am giving you one more chance. Cut that rate down."

ART: I'd answer "Boss,"—and I would say it as nicely as I could—"you have given me a job, and you are telling me I have one more chance. Now I've got to do it my way and not your way. If it is my responsibility to try and cut down the absentee rate, don't tell me how much time I have to do it in. If it is my responsibility, I have got to do it my way."

If managers have delegated functions but are denied discretion to administer them, frustration and dissatisfaction are likely to arise. *"In short the formal organization places the employee in a situation that requires him to behave more and more like an infant; but, of course, while doing this, he is well paid and given seniority and other benefits.*—In short, the organization places the employee in a work situation in which he has little or nothing to say about his goals, the way to achieve his goals and so forth."[13]

We may be developing executives, Professor Argyris goes on to say, "who are primarily directive, hardworking, job oriented, tolerant of frustration and not desirous of focusing on the feelings of others (or their own). Although such executives will *probably get the job done*, there is sound evidence to show that they will *not* tend to develop subordinates into mature leaders."[14]

Professor Argyris is not sure how this dilemma is to be resolved. He suggests that changes in the organizational structure which will modify the work situation need to be made before people are changed.

We do not understand how the organizational structure, the formal organization and division of functions, can be modified without an awareness on the part of executives and top managers that the development of the managerial potential and creativity is the prior step. As a matter of fact, Professor Argyris continues, "Perhaps the most important recommendation, and the one that is most strongly backed up by research, is that executives need to become more aware of themselves *and* the impact of their behavior. This will automatically lead them to being more aware of others because we know that in order to understand others we must first understand ourselves."

This brings us back to the principal thesis of this chapter. The manager's function is to help subordinates within the structure of his organization to develop their potential in carrying forward the objectives of the enterprise. *How* this function is to be accomplished depends upon the manager's increasing understanding of what is involved in learning. We turn, next, to this difficult and complex problem.

NOTES

1. The reader is urged to read the workshop excerpts carefully. Some may find the protocols immoderately long. I ask the reader's indulgence. Close attention to what the several members of the workshop are saying and how they express themselves can help the reader gain insight into how managers can be helped to develop their insights.

2. During World War II, I served as consultant to the personnel division of one of the largest airplane companies in the United States. One of my first responsibilities was to evaluate the work of the division. In examining what was being done, I listed over one hundred different responsibilities being carried out by the department, ranging from issuing coupons for gas rationing, sending flowers to the families of employees who were deceased, checking the number of meals served in the cafeterias and the number of cars entering the parking lots, escorting military personnel on tours through the plants, selling U. S. Bonds to employees, and persuading recalcitrant employees not to quit their jobs.

3. Who is well enough informed or competent or wise enough to lead another person's life? Each of us has his own heart full of aches and his own head full of confusions which keep us busy trying to straighten out our own lives.

4. There are many nonplant problems raised by employees and managers. A large organization may include special employee services to which referral is made. If the organization has no formal setup for such special services, referral can be made to the relevant community agency. My point is that ordinarily it is not the direct responsibility of a manager to deal with nonjob problems of employees.

5. For two rather severe indictments of the movement to teach human relations in industry the reader is referred to an address (in mimeographed form) delivered by Professor Malcolm P. McNair, *What Price Human Relations*, to the Harvard Business School alumni

on June 22, 1956 and to an article by William H. Whyte Jr. which appeared in *Fortune*, June 1956. I sharply disagree with the position taken in these articles.

6. W. J. Goode, and I. Fowler, "Incentive Factors in a Low Morale Plant." *Amer. Sociol. Rev.*, 1949, 14, 618-624. Quoted in A. H. Brayfield, and W. H. Crockett, "Employee Attitudes and Employee Perform-ance," *Psychological Bulletin*, 1955, 52, 396-424. This article examines and summarizes the literature bearing on the relationship between employee attitudes and employee performance. The appended bibliog-raphy lists many important studies of the last few years.

7. Warner, Davis, and Gardner. Quoted in Brayfield and Crockett, *op. cit.*, p. 417.

8. S. Lieberman. Quoted in Brayfield and Crockett, *op. cit.*, p. 420.

9. The point will be fully appreciated if this question is posed: What would the reaction be on the part of corporation executives if the union leadership required managers to attend union sponsored programs in order to enlist their loyalty to the unions?

10. The Amalgamated Clothing Workers and the International Ladies' Garment Workers represent genuine union-management co-operation, to cite two outstanding examples.

11. The reader is undoubtedly acquainted with the literature dealing with the function of staff managers especially in relation to line managers. Confusion is the rule in their interrelations. Staff manager is a counselor, investigator, or analyst who may be called upon for advice or recommendations. *He does not make decisions.* That is the function of line authority. Yet how frequently line managers encourage staff associates to become involved in decision making, and how often staff people fall into this trap of divided authority and responsibility. When something goes wrong the mutual recrimination starts with lowered morale as a consequence. Robert C. Sampson, *The Staff Role in Management* (New York: Harper and Brothers, 1955). Also, J. A. McIntyre, "Personnel Management—What is our Purpose," *Canadian Personnel and Industrial Relations Journal*, January, 1957, p. 7.

12. While one should not make decisions for which he is not respon-sible, he should take the opportunity to develop wider interests which may lead to more responsibility and, hence, wider decisions. This is the basic philosophy of management expressed by William B. Given, Jr., Chairman of the Board, American Brake Shoe Company. "Delega-tion (of authority) is merely the first step which makes it possible for the individual to assume authority. It creates the climate in which he is freed to reach out for still more and more responsibilities, not only in his own bailiwick but also in company areas beyond his own."

"Reaching Out in Management," *Harvard Business Review*, March-April 1952, p. 37. For a full statement see Mr. Given's book, *Bottom-up Management* (New York: Harper and Brothers, 1949).

13. See, Chris Argyris, "Recent Trends in Executive Behavior," *Advanced Management*, March, 1956.

14. Chris Argyris, "Top Management Dilemma: Company Needs *vs.* Individual Development," *Personnel*, Vol. 32, pp. 123-134, September, 1955.

PART II

THE LEARNING PROCESS
FOR MANAGERS

IV

THE NATURE OF LEARNING

ANYONE who undertakes *on a professional level* to help another develop needs to understand what is involved in the teaching-learning process. This should be emphasized in the area of superior-subordinate relations. One gets the impression that every major executive or senior manager considers himself an expert on how to "handle" people. Rarely do they express a real need for their own growth in relating to their subordinates. Sometimes one voices such need but then quickly adds, "I can hardly take the time for this. There are so many important matters which need my attention."

Only a rare and exceptionally wise individual can, without special discipline, help another develop. Most persons have neither the understanding nor the wisdom to engage in this delicate task. The ability to use oneself for the benefit of the learner is difficult to acquire, and it must be learned. Experience or growing older does not in itself yield an understanding of learning any more than eating fifty thousand meals gives one an understanding of the biochemistry of the bile. A knowledge of dietetics and an understanding of food values are required to plan a well-balanced, nourishing diet. An understanding of modern clinical psychology and mental hygiene is essential for the development of managers (or students, children, and teachers).

The problems in personal development and human relations are probably as complex as the relations between the more recently discovered particles of matter and energy. Everyone recognizes the need for specialized study to understand modern relativity physics. Few adults recognize the need for specialized study to understand the complexities of learning.[1]

Many management or supervisory development programs are ineffective because they do not rest squarely on an understanding of what is involved in learning. A case-study program, role playing, workshops, conferences, lectures, audiovisual programs, or any other *technique* will not, in itself, afford an understanding of the learning process.

The content of a management development program must not be confused with the process through which it is being communicated. For the past fifteen years almost all of the effort of management development has gone into building *materials* and discovering *contents* for programs. The time is ripe to pay attention to the *process* through which the materials are communicated and by which they may be assimilated. In a word, *there is a profession of teaching-learning apart from what is being taught.*

Industry does not yet require its managers to learn *how* to help others to learn. Industry does want managers to develop their associates and subordinates. The connection between the two objectives has not yet been made in management circles. Ideally, centers could be established in or out of the industry so that managers might have the opportunity or be required to undertake the study of the teaching-learning process. Until such arrangements are made, managers will have to depend upon irregular, sporadic, one to five day telescoped, quasi-holiday conferences on management development.

The rest of this book offers to the serious student of management development a description of the nature of learning and the complex problems involved. I shall present one specific approach to the problem of the nature of learning.[2] The ideas to be explored are not merely my opinions. The analyses which follow are supported by many psychiatrists, clinical psychologists, child guidance workers, and experienced social workers. Furthermore, they are supported by a rapidly increasing number of educators at all levels of education. It does not follow that these professionals would subscribe to every detail in what is to follow, but undoubtedly they would agree with this approach.[3]

POSITIVE AND NEGATIVE LEARNING

Every adult possesses habits of learning. People do something to and with the experiences to which they are exposed. The first question to explore is the quality of the learning habits of most adults. *The average adult has learned how not to learn.* He has learned how to avoid genuine, positive learning. There is a difference between the kind of learning which arises out of spontaneous curiosity and which satisfies one's positive expression of individual needs, and the kind of learning which is a product of anxiety, apprehensiveness, and fear of disapproval. In one case we gain increase in skill, capacity, and satisfaction in the exercise of our own power. In the other we avoid threat, punishment, and disapproval. Our problem is to trace how it has come about that most adults have learned how to avoid positive learning.

THE ROLE OF ANXIETY

All human beings are biologically similar. We are also psychologically alike in that all of us want to be liked, approved of, and loved. We want to "belong" to others, to be rooted in the affection of the important people in our lives. We want to depend and to rely upon others for many of our wants and needs. We enjoy being like others and doing things for them. In brief, we are gregarious, cooperative, and dependent.

On the other hand, every normal individual possesses wants, needs, drives, attitudes, and sentiments which are peculiarly his own. Indeed such differences are precisely what makes one an individual. Two or more youngsters in a family differ widely in their "temperaments," motor coordination, speed and quality of learning, and so on. The human infant, more so than any other animal, is dependent upon outside help in the early years of development. The significant people in his early life are usually the parents or other adults who substitute for the parents in whole or in part. The developing child needs physical care and psychological direction. The ease with which he assimilates the language, emotions, attitudes, and habits of the significant adults is proverbial, especially during the first year or two.

From the age of two on, striking changes are observed. The child becomes "negative." He begins to assert himself more and more. He wants his own way more often. He starts to explore, to inquire, to create, and to differ with the important adults in his life and with his siblings. He begins to want his *own* way more and more. He discovers that *he* is somebody. He is an individual who differs from others. He has his own independent will.

The child is now faced with a problem which will recur throughout his life. He wants to be like others. He wants the approval of those who love him and whom he loves, but he also wants, at times, to be like himself. He wishes to express his independent, individual needs. What happens at such times when the wishes or demands of others upon whom he depends collide with his needs for expression of self? The child's feelings become ambivalent and the parent becomes insistent. The parent wants his way but the child insists on his own way. The child is full of his own will, and is judged willful by the parent.

Willfulness, in the eyes of the parent, is a moral term of disapprobation. A willful child is a naughty one who must be taught what proper behavior is. The parent punishes the child for his willfulness. The child learns through repeated experiences that if he does things his way when the parents want their way, he gets into trouble. *His* will is something bad, wicked, and is followed by recrimination. In a word, the child experiences anxiety.

We are not concerned here with judging when or where parents should discipline their children. We are not discussing the fact that children need to be directed. We are not pleading for the rights of children to do what they feel like doing when they want to do it. We are simply calling attention to the fact that *children experience anxiety* when the exercise of the independent will is accompanied by punishment, scolding, threat, or deprivation of privilege. More often than not the child does not understand what the parent is *talking* about. Adult patterns and pseudo-logical explanations are a foreign world to the very young. The child hears the loud voice, sees the rigid gestures and flushed face of the adult, and feels the smack. The child experiences *rejection*. He feels insecure and unwanted. He is threatened at the loss of support of those upon whom he depends. His relations to his loved ones are disturbed and, hence, his psychological security is threatened. As a result of many such experiences in the early years of development, *the child associates with his own independent will feelings of anxiety*. Being different—doing things your own way—gets you into trouble. There are dangerous risks involved. You are disapproved.

The child soon learns to play it safe. The way to avoid anxiety, recrimination, and punishment is to adjust to what the significant people around you demand. He ceases to act spontaneously, creatively, and positively. He behaves compulsively and partially to meet threat and to avoid trouble. He learns not to expose his own will in a positive, spontaneous manner, how not to learn in his own way, and how to submit, yield, or withdraw.

Most of this early habit formation occurs on a nonverbal and subconscious level. The child, of course, is not aware of the fact that he experiences anxiety. He does feel threatened and rejected but has no object to attach his anxiety to, other than his "naughty, evil" self.

This is the root of our anxiety over expressing difference and independence in our adult life. Being different involves the risk of social disapproval and recrimination. We learn to play it safe, not to stick out our necks and take chances. We learn to conform. We learn to avoid the conscious reawakening of anxiety feeling and to allay it as we sense it arising.[4]

The fear (anxiety) of social disapproval is carried on outside of the home.[5] The same pattern prevails in our elementary and secondary schools. Instead of the authority of the parents, the school child meets it again in other authoritative figures, the teachers, the principal, and in his own age group. The college instructors or industrial foremen continue the authority pattern. So do the neighbors and "public opinion," the great "it" or "they." We become a nation of conformists, afraid to express our genuine differences in matters important to us. The many kinds of risks are too threatening.

LEARNING IS DISTURBING

Genuine learning requires a change in behavior. A change in behavior necessitates a different organization of our attitudes, feelings, and understanding. One acquires modified or new views regarding traditional ways of behaving. The reorganization of self involves criticism of self. Dissatisfaction with oneself leads to uncomfortable feelings of guilt. We experience annoyance, irritation, inadequacy, doubt, and confusion.

No one ordinarily enjoys such experiences. Each of us has developed an involved system of defenses against facing inevitable conflict between outward conformity and independent need for self-expression. The ambivalence and conflict we experience over denying that at times our needs are different cannot evaporate.

If we are too dependent upon others, or too often submit or conform to the demands others make upon us, we experience hostility and/or frustration. We dislike being "yes men." A point is reached, every now and then, when we refuse to go along, and we speak our piece or act independently. Our declaration of independence is immediately followed by fear of the consequences which are likely to follow. We have "put our foot" in it. We feel scared or guilty at having dared to be different. Now we turn around and try to make up. We want to be in the good graces of the other. We become dependent again.

Thus we are inevitably caught in the swings or cycles of acting dependently and independently. When the balance is too far out on either side we experience annoyance, irritation, frustration, hostility, guilt, or confusion in various degrees. The more significant the situation, the more involved we are, the sharper is the disturbance.

Any living situation is much more complex than this description indicates. No one is ever concerned with merely one series of relations to other people or one problem. How we act toward, and react to, each other and to situations depends upon thousands of different patterns that have been built up over the years. Feelings are never simple and clear-cut.

If a superior accuses a subordinate of a misdeed, the subordinate may feel indignation because the charge is unjustified, or shame and indignation because there is some basis for the charge. Again, the subordinate may have been innocent this time but has, in the past, misbehaved. He will now feel justified in resenting the scolding but part of him will sense the justification of the charge for past deeds. In trying to decide how to react the employee feels "mixed up." He is hostile and wants to fight back and justify himself. He is also afraid that his aggression may lead to further argument and serious consequences. He may endanger either his promotion or the increase in salary. What will his friends say if he does not get the promotion? An explanation to his wife of what happened will cause another series of arguments, and she will not invite his parents over for dinner as they had planned. On the other hand, he is tired of the job anyway. He knows of an opportunity to work for another company. He might move faster there. But you never know. He might not get the job and he has one now. After all, he's been with this company for eight years and his present superior won't remain in that job forever. Maybe he should keep quiet or try to find a good explanation for what happened? Perhaps blame someone else? Maybe the boss is right? Maybe he did mess things up? Perhaps he's not as smart as he thought he was?

The focal disturbance experienced at any given time is the *net product* of many kinds of likes, dislikes, uncertainties, fears, joys, expectancies, hostilities, dependencies, risks, and the need for self-expression. Feelings are at cross-purposes, and one is not certain about what to do or say.

Each of us has lived through experiences like this more than once. We subtly rehearsed the alternatives, the risks, and experience the anxiety, fears, and confusions within split seconds and decide upon an answer. We decide to try to avoid the threat or to admit the failure or to express indignation at an injustice. In any case we learn, either negatively or positively. And in any case *we are disturbed*. Something is at stake. We are involved. There can be no change without disturbance.[6]

RESISTANCE

A normal person does not enjoy being psychologically disturbed and emotionally upset. Change requires self-criticism, painful self-disapproval, and, sometimes, the acceptance of social disapproval. The pretty picture we have built up of ourselves is discovered to be false. It isn't comfortable to discover our defenses and the innumerable pretensions we practice to conceal from others and ourselves what we are really like. We resist change to avoid disturbance.

Resisting change, however, increases disturbance. Further defenses and pretensions are called for. The first lie calls for a second, the second for a third. Most resistance to change does not occur on a conscious level. Each of us has developed innumerable ways of avoiding self-criticism and facing conflict directly and openly. Conflicts cannot be done away with as long as man has to learn. They can be met openly or dealt with subconsciously. What are some of the ways through which we try to disguise, conceal, distort, or deny inner conflicts?

Compulsive drinking (alcohol), compulsive gambling, and compulsive eating are widespread phenomena. Individuals behaving in this manner are trying to deny or to escape difficulties with which they seem unable or unwilling to cope. They are trying to obtain surcease and temporary satisfaction to allay a gnawing sense of unrest and anxiety.

Criticizing other people to avoid responsibility is another form of resistance to change, a way of covering up guilt we might otherwise experience. Gossip, prejudice—racial or religious—are indulged in, since running someone else down gives one a specious sense of security. If someone is worse than I am, then, at least, I am better than someone else. Another form of escaping from oneself, of running away from the risks of being different and becoming disturbed, is to conform to the patterns of one's associates, that is to say, "public opinion." Our success is usually measured against what our friends value and what accords with their status.

Success may have many meanings. In our society it means, primarily, financial prestige. Money, along with the power and possessions it commands, determines one's important status. The possession of wealth is taken as proof of achievement. The competitive striving for financial success means that one has to win over others. The competitor experiences hostility and isolation (which is often not consciously recognized). This, in turn, generates feelings of anxiety which must be allayed by more competitive striving. Not many of us realize that by manipulating others we are manipulating ourselves. We resist facing our basic insecurity since self-exposure is painful. Instead we redouble our efforts to triumph over others, seeking to reassure ourselves that we are someone.

Resistance to change takes many forms. One of the chief weapons to combat change in oneself is language. Given enough words and the *ability to express* them, we can talk our way into or out of any situation. The technical term for this is *rationalization*. We argue from feeling to fact, not the other way around. It isn't difficut to find many good reasons for saying or doing what we do. If we don't find them we can readily discover or create them. The real reasons had better not be discussed.

Casual observation of one's own talk or that of others will convince the reader of the enormous amount of energy we expend in justifying or defending our own point of view.

Really to understand what another is trying to communicate involves an effort that few of us are willing to make. First, the listener must avoid moral judgment, at least before the speaker has expressed himself. Second, the listener should make every effort to comprehend what the speaker means, not what the listener wants him to mean.

Ordinarily, we do not listen patiently and sympathetically to a different point of view making certain we understand before we answer. We have an answer in the air before the other has finished. Listen to the pitch of voices, observe the facial and bodily gestures of the speakers. Each wants to control the other, to dominate, to win. This is no less true if the pitch of voice is restrained and the language polite.

Few of us welcome challenge to change. It means an admission of something unsatisfactory in ourselves. This is irritating, confusing, and disturbing if the issue is vital to us. It seems easier to remain as one is and to resist change. We resist the threat of discomfort not realizing that basically we are adding to our load of insecurity. We are escaping from ourselves, denying the right to create, the joy of growth following the pain of learning.

Double talk is not confined to our communication with others. The individual double talks to himself to resist the disturbance of change and to escape the accompanying reorganization of self. This process is easily observed when we "determine" to start dieting or to stop smoking—tomorrow morning. The pie *à la môde* in front of us or the tasty cigarette at hand is not resisted. That is precisely what we now want. What is resisted is the change in habit. The "determination" to abstain is reduced to another futile verbal promise to ourselves. By promising to stop tomorrow we pretend not to have our pie although we eat it. We talk ourselves into believing that we really are going to start the diet after this one last indulgence. And it is so easy to find a reason to postpone the starting (double talk).

Less easily observed are the subtle self-deceptions engaged in during reflection when we defend or justify our behavior in an important situation. To admit failure, to face inadequacy, to accept genuine self-criticism and responsibility for change in vitally important matters is not easy.

THE REDUCTION OF FEAR AND ANXIETY

Man requires wisdom through affliction; we learn through experience only if we use our experiences to learn. We become wise or mature as we struggle with the inevitable and never-ending problem of balancing our need to live with others and our pressing need to be individual.

Finding and redefining balance is the lever of growth. The tentative balances are found in *living* situations compounded of degrees of uncertainty, fear, guilt, dependence, love, hostility, resistance, aggression, independence, knowledge, understanding, misunderstanding, fear of disapproval, and the seeking of approval.

Every individual struggles to create his own syntheses or to resist creating anything of his own. The most important contribution that can be made by anyone close to the learner is to encourage the latter to create, to learn positively. The best way to do this is to remove the threat of recrimination, reprisal, or disapproval.

Every learner must struggle with his own ambivalence, his own dissatisfaction, and the guilt and fear generated by them. This is difficult enough without adding to the struggle the additional fears and anxieties and disapprovals induced by significant people in the life of the learner.

The learner is more likely to struggle with himself if he does not feel compelled to direct his struggle against others. He will then be engaged in constructive learning for himself instead of learning how to avoid the disapproval of others.

THE REMAKING OF EXPERIENCE

Significant learning, that is, learning which makes a difference in one's behavior, is not additive but integrative. One does not learn in any vital sense by adding fact upon fact. What kind of learning would it be to memorize, for no special reason, all of the names, addresses, and telephone numbers listed under the letter "A" in the local telephone directory?

On the other hand, one would find it helpful to make a special effort and select out of the directory the telephone numbers of friends or merchants or physicians that one calls often or is likely to want to reach in an emergency. The *selective use* of such numbers fits in with special, meaningful, purposive (integrated) behavior.

Let us carry this analogy further. Suppose you have mechanically memorized *all* the numbers under letter "A." When or why do you call any particular number? The data you possess, that is, the names and telephone numbers, will not give the answer to this question. The specific number you call and the timing of the call have little to do with the number listing. What you are experiencing and your need to interact with and to integrate your experience as you meet a changing situation (the need for a doctor or the fire department or a friend or to place a meat order) determine *which* number you will select.

The popular idea that learning is a process of storing data and the more data one has the more learning one possesses is false. Facts are assimilated, integrated in relation to the ongoing experience of the learner. Seeing interrelationships, readjusting and modifying behavior, is the essence of learning. To learn is to re-shape, to re-form, and to re-make one's experience.

In the following chapter we shall explore more fully how one is helped to learn in this vital sense of learning.

NOTES

1. All of us have heard and told many stories about psychiatrists, the specialists in understanding personality development. Usually the point of the story is an attack on psychiatry or it pokes fun at the psychiatrist. I suspect this is our layman's compensation. We discharge our uneasiness about the psychiatrists' superior knowledge about us or/and the insecurity we feel about our own knowledge of ourselves.

2. No one is more aware than I am of the dangers of oversimplification of the ideas to be presented. I am not presenting a definitive analysis of what is involved in learning. The concepts selected for analysis, such as "rejection," "will," "guilt," and "dependence," do no

more than point to modes or levels of experience. Each one of the concepts covers large areas which need to be explored and charted. Professor Gardner Murphy writes, "Psychology is in about the same position today as chemistry was in Boyle's time." *Personality* (New York: Harper and Brothers, 1947), p. 914.

3. The reader who wishes to pursue the problem of the nature of learning will find a detailed analysis in the following works by the author. *The Dynamics of Learning*, 3rd edition (210 Ellicott Street, Buffalo: H. Stewart and Company, 1956); *The Teaching-Learning Process*, (New York: Dryden Press, 1953); *Learning Through Discussion* (438 Delaware Avenue, Buffalo: Human Relations for Industry, 1951).

4. The foregoing analysis of anxiety as arising out of the interpersonal relations with the significant people in our early years is supported by the clinical experiences and writings of H. Mowrer, E. Fromm, R. May, K. Horney, Miller and Dollard, H. Sullivan, and K. Goldstein, among others. Their chief publications are:

O. H. Mowrer, *Learning Theory and Personality Dynamics* (New York: Ronald Press, 1950).

E. Fromm, "Selfishness and Self-Love," *Psychiatry*, November 1939.

———, *Escape From Freedom*.

———, *Man For Himself* (New York: Rinehart, 1947).

Rollo May, *The Meaning of Anxiety* (New York: Ronald Press, 1950).

———, *Man's Search For Himself* (New York: W. W. Norton, 1953).

K. Horney, *The Neurotic Personality of Our Time* (New York: W. W. Norton, 1937).

J. Dollard, and N. E. Miller, *Personality and Psychotherapy* (New York: McGraw-Hill 1950).

H. S. Sullivan, *The Interpersonal Theory of Psychiatry* (New York: W. W. Norton, 1953).

K. Goldstein, *The Organism* (New York: American Book Co., 1939). *Human Nature in The Light of Psychopathology* (Cambridge, Mass.: Harvard University Press, 1940).

5. Fear is to be distinguished from anxiety. Fear can usually be attached to a conscious focus. We fear being burned, being hit by speeding automobiles, being punished for an act we know is wrong. Anxiety is felt when *there is no awareness* of what it is that bothers us.

6. This does not mean that one learns when confusion or disturbance is present. No learning occurs without disturbance. However, one can experience disturbance without learning.

V

LEARNING TO LEARN

NEW WAYS OF THINKING AND FEELING

IN THIS chapter I shall assume that the manager functions as a leader of his immediate group. He works on a group or individual basis. He may act as leader of discussions with his subordinates or he may meet with any one of them for private conferences. In either case the manager, who wants to help others learn, needs to obtain a realistic view of himself and his associates as they react in the teaching-learning process, and he needs to be exposed to an unconventional kind of thinking and feeling which contradicts "the organization man's" quest for normalcy and adaptability.[1]

To characterize the dynamic processess in the teaching-learning situation, I have selected four important aspects illustrating the new ways of thinking and feeling with which skilled managers should become familiar. What constitutes an answer to an important question raised by a learner? How does one react to conflict and difference? What if an individual does not want to learn? Finally, what is consensus, and is it desirable?

Before turning to the specific discussion of these four areas I should like to comment generally on five different levels which exist in a teaching-learning group experience, namely, the social, ethical, psychological, scientific, and professional.

THE MULTIDIMENSIONAL CONTEXTS OF LEARNING[2]
SOCIAL NORMS

When two or more persons meet, there can be no communication between them unless they share certain values. Social relations as opposed to chance physical contact imply that individuals possess expectations regarding one another's behavior. Manager and subordinates hold certain expectations in common and differ in others. There is some common ground in a discussion of religion, for example, yet the discussers may be members of different churches or religions or even be nonbelievers.

A perceptive manager will become increasingly aware of the expectations of the group he leads and of what he expects as he leads them. I speak now of his *awareness*, not of his judging the desirability or wrongness of the expectations. It is normal for a manager to be aware of his status and position. He expects to behave toward his subordinates and in certain situations as others expect him to behave. Traditionally, the manager is expected to possess superior knowledge and he believes, or is expected to pretend, that he does. It is understood generally that the manager can issue orders and determine policy. That is what being a manager means. He is in control and others look to him for direction. He leads, the subordinates follow.

This is a normal managerial and subordinate expectation. In acquiring new ways of relating to the learner the manager can neither ignore the normal expectations nor fully accept them. He has to be aware of the different norms which are operating and of the altered ones involved in learning and changing. How this dilemma is to be resolved is part of skilled leadership, as we shall see.

ETHICAL ASSUMPTIONS

Our culture teaches us to conform to a series of religious and ethical beliefs. These are the absolutes of our society. Our ideals of Justice, Truth, and Goodness are so taken for granted in our literature, official utterances, secular schooling, and religious instruction that it requires considerable cultural sophistication to recognize the arbitrary character of these usually unexamined premises. These sacred and taken-for-granted beliefs and ideals, how they have come about, how they function, how they help or hinder the objectives of managerial development, must be recognized by the manager. This is the central thesis of Mr. William H. Whyte's disturbing study, *The Organization Man*. Managers and candidates for executive positions are the leaders and victims of a new social ethic which requires them to conform to the group, to adapt to the group norms. It is not merely the conformity which is dangerous, according to Mr. Whyte. It is the fact that the managers believe it is morally imperative that the individual should learn or be taught to conform for his own good. "Belongingness," "consensus," loyalty to the organization, getting along with everybody, and being "well-rounded," these are the new, unexamined, much-needed goals of modern life.

Mr. Whyte makes explicit a view and a basic ethic which is creeping up on us but of which we are unaware. A manager who is trying to develop the creativity of his subordinates through the usual, unexamined management development manuals or packaged programs at universities or company conferences will be shocked when, and if, he discovers the subtle manipulation of his subordinates which he is practicing and the goal of conformity toward which he is moving, along with his subordinates.

I am not now concerned with what the manager does once he discovers the unstated ethical assumptions through and with which he and his group are working. It is important that everybody concerned in developing managers become aware of the presence of accepted ethical ideals. They have to be taken into account in any plan for modifying them or substituting different ideals. One's sacred beliefs must be understood and appreciated, not condemned, if the believer is expected to examine them with a view toward possible change. The helper starts where the learner is, not where the helper would like him to be. The manager, no less than his subordinates, professes loyalty to the group's ideals and recognizes the gaps between belief and practice, the contradictions, and the inconsistencies. Trying to be helpful does not mean that the manager calls attention to the disparity between cherished belief and ignored practice. The manager is not a preacher. He is an analyst. He realizes that the application of ideals in specific situations is trying and, often, has to be qualified and compromised by mutually exclusive objectives. To the perceptive manager Principles are reduced to principles.

PSYCHOLOGICAL NEEDS

This dimension is little understood. In every learning experience, the helper must become sensitized to his own feelings toward the learners. What use does he make of himself for the benefit of the learner? What needs of his own are being fulfilled or frustrated? What are his biases which color his interpretations and distort his perceptions? The manager is hard put to discover the feelings of the members toward each other, toward him, and in relation to the content. What do they really want in these meetings? Are they communicating or are they engaging in the usual folderol of pleasant amenities with no one in danger of being hurt?

Most of us fear to examine these pretty pictures of ourselves and the pretty language with which we so clearly and simply describe our opinions, judgments, beliefs, and excellent reasons for acting as we do. He who examines himself and others (in a healthy frame of mind because he wants to understand and improve himself) is embarking on a dangerous journey. It is hard to predict where this examination will lead.

No manager can become skilled in developing others without long and laborious self-examination. This dimension of the personality needs of manager and learner cannot be ignored. I shall return to the discussion of these issues in the next two chapters.

THE SCIENCE OF HUMAN EMOTIONS

Management development is not magical. If an interview between the manager and an individual or a conference between leader and group has a sense of direction, a purpose, and a structure, one should be able to describe it. This does not mean the description will adequately cover all of the dimensions. It does mean that one should be able to state the assumptions upon which one is carrying out the process, the results which follow, whether one can predict general uniformities, and whether certain principles of helping others can be communicated and further tested. There is little precise knowledge about how people learn, how groups operate, and how one teaches. People do differ in teaching skills and in learning potential. Except in the rare case, skills are developed and learning is facilitated. There have been some great natural teachers and some insatiable learners. The majority of teachers, however, must acquire ability, and the majority of learners must be helped to develop. True, the knowledge is not precise, but it is better to possess what little is known than to move in darkness.

It is a serious mistake to believe that anyone is qualified to manage others (in the area of development of potential) without the available understanding of what is involved in helping others.

The various methods and contents of managerial development programs are based upon certain assumptions, expressed or implied, regarding how people learn. Thus we have the case method approach, the conference, role playing, the incident approach, audiovisual techniques, job rotation, and individual interviewing. No one method, content, or combination is objectionable in itself. What is troublesome and misleading is dogmatic insistence on clichés and rules and verbal principles. Many managers, unsure of themselves and of what they are doing, seek security through the *Word*, through half-baked knowledge.

It is important that inquiry and research into how people learn and develop be supported. Without this knowledge the exercise of skill becomes personal idiosyncrasy. The leader or manager who seems to be consistently helpful will be exercising great skill, that is, he will possess the best available knowledge and will understand how inadequate it is. The skilled leader understands that even if our knowledge of human relations were more reliable and valid the logic of ideas rarely parallels the lust for living. The manager discovers what is "wrong" with an associate. He knows what "should" be done. It is a wise manager who keeps that knowledge to himself until such time as the associate wants to, or is helped to become ready to, avail himself of the manager's wisdom. The manager's knowledge has become a bit of manager wisdom in the curing process.

THE PROFESSIONAL LEVEL

The activities which constitute a management development program point to a goal, the development of the individuals, the present and future managers of the organization. What that goal should be, a well-rounded team member or a brilliant deviate, is another matter. In any case, there is a purpose which the leader and his organization want to achieve. How is such purpose most effectively achieved? By distributing outlines which list the characteristics of a good manager? By presenting communications or human relations or meeting change manuals? By pleasant intellectual exchanges of the several "ideas" found in the manuals which everyone finds "interesting" and "enjoyable," and more of which should be provided at follow-up conferences?

Unless the manager operates on a professional level, little will be accomplished. By professional level I do not mean that every helpful manager must be a certified psychiatrist or clinical psychologist. This might make matters worse. By professional I mean the leader's understanding of how to use himself in the learning situation to carry out the function delegated to him by his organization. I shall return to a detailed examination of this in the next two chapters.

The professional manager gains increasing insight and skill in moving from one level to another. The social norms of the members, the ethical absolutes, the psychological needs of leader and participants, the knowledge which orders and structures what is happening, these dimensions and their impact upon the goal of developing managers for the organization constitute the matrix in which change and learning take place. No one dimension can be ignored. Someone must be aware of the uncertainties, complexities, and partial resolutions which all will experience. Someone must be in control of what is happening so that the experiences will have focus and direction. Someone must possess the humility to appreciate and accept the fact that genuine learning is difficult, painful, and slow because so many levels are involved. This is the burden of and the challenge to the professional manager.

Having presented some idea of the multidimensional context of learning, I shall now return to several areas which will illustrate, through actual verbatim reports of a workshop, how the dimensions interweave. The purpose of this presentation, I repeat, is to help the reader become more deeply involved in new approaches to learning.

WHAT IS AN ANSWER?

The problems which can be answered are relatively unimportant; the truly significant questions of human life admit no final answers. The different religious and philosophic systems evidence the poetic effort to come to grips with the essential meaning of our lives which remains, nevertheless, as mysterious as ever.

European tradition, through the development of science, has succeeded in accumulating a vast knowledge about many matters which *describes* the ways in which facts are systematically related to each other. Such descriptions consist of mathematical equations and have little bearing on the basic values, beliefs, and hopes of man. "Gravitational geometric fields," hold the physical universe together, but passion, love, and curiosity bind or split the world of man.

Logic and mathematics do not begin to exhaust the nature of reality. Yet most of us have grown up in the tradition that the solution to human problems is found in statements, logical propositions. Our formal education is primarily intellectual. We learn answers, general propositions, abstract concepts. We accumulate facts, but continue behaving pretty much the same as the generations of biblical times. Knowledge does not seem to make much difference. The confused world in which we of the latter part of the twentieth century live is grim testimony to this statement. We have not learned how to live together well, either on a small community basis or on an international scale.

Peace of mind cannot be purchased by the investment of three or four dollars in a book which claims to supply the answers. It costs a great deal more to discover one's answers to one's problems.

The problem which concerns us, in the present context, however, is that of indicating how managers in industry might be helped to discover answers for the complexities involved in developing themselves as managers and of helping others to assume more responsibility in their industrial obligations.

An answer to a specific problem requires a recognition (dimension of science) of the factors involved. Analysis, ordinarily, is helpful in locating the source of the problem and in defining alternative steps which may lead to a resolution of the difficulty. This is merely the first step. What one wants to do, however, is not simply a matter of knowledge or analysis. What one *does* occurs in a complicated context of hope, fear, risk, courage, resistance, guilt, rationalization, confusion, ambivalence, and so on (dimensions of norms, ethical beliefs, and personal needs). It is a spectrum of feeling which eventuates in the drive or will or motivation which is the decision. To escape from the discomfort of struggle, to avoid the disagreeable feelings of uncertainty, inadequacy, and self-responsibility, we turn to the expert, the formula, the book, the superior, or *the* verbal answer. Thus we think we avoid the heartache and headache of assuming responsibility for our own decision. We run out on ourselves and avoid the inner struggle which alone supplies a meaningful resolution, however temporary and partial, to *our* problem. Answers are, by definition, verbal propositions, statements, abstractions. The application of the answer requires a commitment, a bit of living with its accompanying disturbance, risk, and reorganization of feeling.

Here are two excerpts. One is taken from the first of twelve two-hour sessions, the other from the last session. Note that the leader refrains from giving answers and helps the several members to assume the burden of exploring their own questions:

LEADER: What are some of the problems you'd like to discuss?

BEN: A manager must be a good salesman. To be a leader you have to sell yourself.

BILL: That's right. No matter what group you are in charge of you have something to sell.

JERRY: That's true enough. But how do you do it?

LEADER: Tell me, Jerry, how do you propose to find out?

JERRY: Why, that's why I'm here listening to you.

LEADER: You mean I'm supposed to be an expert on this selling business?

JERRY: That's a good way to put it.

LEADER: I'm afraid I have nothing to sell.

DICK: You're selling yourself now. That's a skilled quality of salesmanship you are employing. Your technique is a bit different, that's all. (A long period of silence.)

DICK: What's the purpose of our being here? Aren't you supposed to tell us what makes a good manager?

LEADER: I thought *we* were to discuss what makes a good manager.

WILL: Well, a good manager changes ideas or attitudes.

LEADER: And how does he do that?

GEORGE: I've taught "J" courses until I was blue in the face. Nothing much happens. I've taught human relations courses for years and the supervisors go away from the meeting having learned nothing. I guess I've been doing something wrong but I don't know what it is.

PETE: I think the trouble is that we don't give supervisors specific techniques. They can get the right attitudes but they don't know how to use them.

DAVE: Isn't it the other way around? If we gave the supervisors the right attitudes, the techniques would be easy to find.

JERRY: (Turning to Leader.) I'd like to hear what you think.

LEADER: You mean about what comes first, attitudes or techniques?

JERRY: No, about how a manager sells himself.

LEADER: I wonder, Jerry, if we shouldn't try to answer Dave's question first?

ED: I think I can answer it. I've always made it a point to structure every meeting I've had with supervisors. I present a technique, then the supervisor applies it under supervision, and then there is a follow up.

LEADER: Do you agree? (The question, addressed to the group, was followed by a long silence.)

LEADER: Can anyone repeat what Ed said? (No one was able to.)

LEADER: I wonder why no one was able to repeat what was said by Ed?

JERRY: I guess we weren't listening.

LEADER: Apparently what you heard was not significant to you? (Silence.)

LEADER: Has anyone learned anything this morning?

JERRY: Not a thing so far as I'm concerned. (Laughter.)

GEORGE: I wouldn't say that. Something is happening to me but I don't know what it is. I'm certainly mixed up and feel very uncomfortable. I have a feeling that you are deliberately not giving us any answers and I'd like to understand that.

The twelfth meeting:

JERRY: Whatever we acquire we acquire through our own effort.

GEORGE: If we hadn't been at these meetings, we would never have understood the book we read.[3] We had to live through some of the experiences we had and convince ourselves.

ED: I see now that what you did during the last few minutes was to put into words what we ourselves were feeling.

JERRY: We had expected you to tell us and we looked to your superior knowledge. We tried to make an expert out of you. I certainly see now that communicating conviction is not giving answers but helping others in the struggle they are having to find out for themselves.

GEORGE: It's too bad we can't live this way in all of our relations. If more people understood that they have to find all of their own answers by themselves we'd have a new kind of relationship everywhere.

PETE: The key as I see it is to help people become involved in what bothers them and not to take away *their* problem by giving them *your* answers.

JERRY: In short, we're all mixed up and we've got to unmix ourselves. Finding proper balances is the rub and it's not comfortable. You have to fight with yourself.

Even a superficial reading of these two excerpts reveals the different quality in the group's understanding at the start and at the close of the sessions of how one finds a meaningful answer. Answers are found in struggling with oneself.

THE ACCEPTANCE OF CONFLICT

Traditionally, we learn *not* to learn. We want to be given answers to avoid the discomfort involved in self-discovery. Finding tentative resolutions to one's problems requires considerations of mutually exclusive needs, desires, and interests. Choosing one alternative compels the rejection of others. In the act of choosing, doubt as to the wisdom or expediency of the choice is not sealed off. One feels ambivalent, uncertain, afraid, militant, defensive, and hopeful.

To be in doubt, to be ambivalent, to see opposing aspects of truth, is to be in pieces. The individual wishes to feel whole, untroubled, and rid of disturbance. Change, however, requires change in previous organization. This must, inevitably, give rise to discomfort and conflict. To learn to accept and use conflict is not easy. The attempt to avoid its acceptance leads to increased conflict.

To be responsible for one's own decisions means to be self-critical, to admit one is not sure of one's self, to assume the risks of error, and to possess the courage of failure. To be responsible means to be an individual and to face the disapproval of nonconformity.

The following exchange reveals how the participants are beginning to realize that answers are found through working out one's own problems:

FRED: One has to understand oneself, one's own insecurities and fears, so that one is able to enter into the similar experiences of others.

CHARLES: How does one do that?

BOB: One way certainly is by going through what we are going through during these meetings.

FRED: It is not merely a matter of reading the material but becoming involved in the ideas, really becoming annoyed and irritated. Doesn't everything we read enter into our growth?

BILL: Not unless you put ideas to work in living situations and sweat it through.

HERB: There must be an understanding of your own motives. I am thinking of one important problem, namely, we must understand our terrific need for attention from others.

DON: I think we have to take a close look at our resistance and how we fight against new ideas and people.

LEADER: How is one helped to look at one's resistance?

FRED: Someone who understands people must be around to give professional help.

BILL: I can give an example of what has happened here. I have learned, for example, that I punish my child because I am annoyed not because I want to help him. The other day we wanted to send our boy to Sunday School. He was getting religion for *us*. He was slow in dressing so I shook him to hurry him along. I think next time I'll shake him less and myself a bit more.

BOB: Bill, you're getting a little relief from your guilt over what you did to the kid.

BILL: That's exactly what my speech meant.

REDIRECTING RESISTANCE

The easiest way to meet change is not to change. At least, so it seems. When someone talks *to* us we usually hear what we want to hear or interpret what we hear to our liking. Similarly, we select and remember from what we read that which fits in with the way we feel and think.

This is a classic example of resistance to change. We choose not to pay attention to items which will be disturbing.[4] The disturbance will stem from our own self-criticism or from social disapproval. In either case dissatisfaction will accompany the intrapersonal experience of moving from one personal organization to another. To modify or change ideas, beliefs, and feelings, which had been a taken-for-granted part of one's self, means that one is willing to admit he is not quite the person he thought he was. We are not referring to the hollow cliché, "Live and learn," or the innocuous "Nobody is perfect" routine. Most of this is idle chatter and a common form of resistance to change.

Significant, vital learning is gut (meaning intestinal) learning. One is tied in knots and must be willing to unravel the rope even as it becomes more tangled in the unraveling. This process of learning requires persistent effort, fighting off disesteem, spotting rationalizations, avoiding finding fault with someone else or some situation, avoiding self-pity and self-justification. It is easy to understand why one resists change. No one wants to deny his wisdom and his feeling of rightness.

Managers, on all levels, fight changing themselves, as do the rest of us. They, too, want to control. They want to "help" others, that is, have them accept the views of managers. Respect for the subordinate turns out to be the self-respect of the manager. "Do it my way, view it through my eyes, and you will develop into a better employee or manager."

The manager is committed to encourage the growth of others. The assumption is that he has something to offer. He must, inevitably, offer himself, what he basically feels and believes. Here is a dilemma. The manager, who wants to help the other in accord with what he, the manager, wants is controlling not helping the other toward discovery of self. Yet the manager who encourages the other to learn must, perforce, offer himself. How can this be resolved?

The manager not only does but also professionally should stand for what he believes. To deny this is to distort reality. What he stands for, what he believes in, is his difference which he is willing to share with the one he helps, *if the latter decides to share.* The manager challenges with his difference not in order to control but to help. To stand by and permit the learner to reject, to resist the proffered help, is an extraordinary achievement on the manager's part. This is one of the important growing points for any manager.

By struggling with his own need to control the learner, the manager learns better to control himself. In this process he is remaking himself. The tendency is for the manager to become impatient when the learner's response is slow or negative. He is likely to think something must be wrong with the learner. This, more likely, is the manager's resistance to learning about his need to win, to dominate. If he recognizes this resistance, he is learning to learn.

The manager who appreciates the resistance to change in himself will recognize it in those he is trying to help. The subordinate or assistant wants to remain the same and will struggle *against* anyone or anything seeking to change him. If, however, no one insists on imposing a foreign will upon him but merely presents another viewpoint for consideration, there is nothing to fight against. There is simply no fight since no one has to win.

Everyone has had the experience of initially disagreeing or differing with another person. If that person indicates respect for your own position and your right to differ, you are likely to feel kindly and warm toward him. Furthermore, you are willing to reexamine your own position and his, since you are not being criticized for your views. There is a kind of yielding, a temporary suspension of self-righteousness and self-justification. One feels understood by the other and, therefore, drawn toward him. Feeling less threatened, and, less defensive, one can afford to examine the challenge being presented.

In such a relatively permissive climate the learner need not use his energy to fight off a foreign will. He uses an awakened curiosity or uncertainty or doubt or annoyance to question himself. He wonders about himself. Since whatever tentative conclusions he reaches will be understood, and *he remains free from attack or disapproval*, he can try to learn rather than to conform or to defend himself because of fear of consequences.

The following exchange shows how the leader challenges several members of the group to help them explore their own attitudes and to give them the opportunity to redirect their thinking if they want to:

TED: The problem of member participation troubles me. It seems to me talking as such isn't important. The member should be involved. He shouldn't answer because he's been put on the spot. I do that and if I get everybody to talk I consider the meeting a good one. I'm beginnning to think that's phony. I think that if any member talks when he's not really interested either the group or the leader should call a halt. And likewise the silent ones should not be forced to come in. (At this point several members glanced at Bob who had said very little.)

LEADER: Bob will bear this out, I think. If I recall correctly Bob attended a workshop about a year ago and for reasons of his own, which are solely his business, he chose not to speak much, as he had the right to.

BOB: You'll never know how scared I was then. I was afraid of what you and the other fellows would think of me. I wasn't sure of myself. But something has happened to me in the past year. I've gotten some insight, I think, and I really want to improve as a discussion leader.

TED: Here's a case in point. You didn't force Bob to speak, you encouraged him to.

CHARLES: What's wrong with going after a guy who talks all the time, or never talks. (Charles quickly glanced at Ted.) Being nice all of the time becomes a bit sickening. My experience is that adults can take it.

LEADER: Ted, I think, didn't like what Charlie said.

TED: I certainly didn't. He made me feel guilty because I had gone after people and now I think it's wrong.

LEADER: I wonder if you're a little mad at Charlie, too.

TED: I am. I think, Charlie, you are now where I was until I got here. You are worried whether you can get everybody into the act so that you can feel you've had a successful meeting. The conference becomes yours, not the members'. (Silence.)

LEADER: Charlie?

CHARLES: Yeah, I'm beginning to see what Ted means.

The leader gave Bob, Ted, and Charles an opportunity to express themselves. Bob and Ted were left free to comment or not since the remarks of the leader were made to the group as a whole. The leader simply called Charles by name inquiring whether he wanted to rejoin to Ted's statement.

There are no definite rules for the leader's use of the idea of challenge. The intensity, time, and manner of challenge depend upon the interpersonal relations of all members of the group. The closer the members feel toward each other and the leader the more direct can the challenge become. Timid members or aggressive participants have to be challenged differently. Again, the degree of challenge will depend upon the participants' readiness to accept the challenge. These variables need to be considered by the leader who is aware of the nature of resistance to learning:

LEADER: Are we ready to go on with challenge?

FERN: Are you challenging us now?

LEADER: Yes. (Laughter.)

TED M.: When I challenge I find that I am merely a devil's advocate. The difference is not a real conviction on my part.

TED B.: In my first three sessions with my group I left the group alone completely. I was afraid to say anything. Then I turned right around and got myself into trouble because I argued for my position.

TED M.: I have lost confidence in challenging professionally because my challenge isn't a real part of my difference.

ART: You can sometimes introduce an artificial difference in order to obtain discussion.

TED M.: I think the difference has got to be a sincere one. The group will sense superficiality or artificiality. I think one of the troubles with me is that I am afraid to say "I don't know the answer." When the group is silent I start running with the ball in circles or in the wrong direction.

ART: How often I have done that, too! From what I see now, if the members of your group are talked out and you still have one half hour or forty-five minutes left, I would say if nothing further is brought up, quit for the day.

GORDON: At that point I would feel lost, but would not want to let on that I was.

LEADER: I wonder if every group would not respond to something like this. "Look fellows, I'm all mixed up like you. I don't know what is the matter, why are all of us bogged down? Can you help me and can we help each other?" Don't you think almost every normal group would rise to that kind of challenge?

TED M.: Being superficial is not being real. Unless you are all mixed up I don't think you should say it.

TED B.: You can't just let yourself go and be sincere. Along with sincerity has to go a professional understanding of what's going on.

LEADER: Ted, isn't our point now what the leader does when he is lost and doesn't know what's going on? Would not it be better to be yourself than to try to fake?

ART: The more the professional cloak shows, the more you need a new tailor. You are best in performance when your technique doesn't show.

LEADER: You mean, Art, the leader doesn't say in so many words, feeling that there is another hour assigned, "What do you fellows want now?" You mean, Art, he is going through the motions there, and really is not interested in helping the group?

ART: That's right.

A short time later:

TED M.: I haven't said anything yet this morning. I want to ask a question now. Haven't you been lecturing more than usual this morning?

LEADER: Yes, I am pushing a bit now. Maybe I am making a mistake. What does the group think?

TED M.: Maybe I should not have asked my question?

LEADER: Why not? It was a good question.

BOB: I'm still struggling with the concept of "frustration."

CHARLES: It seems to me frustration ties in with having to win. If you have to win and you don't you are bound to be frustrated.

TED B.: Why is it that all of us have to win most of the time?

GORDON: No one wants to be last in the league.

ART: No one wants to be, but it would be a fine balance if we accepted that fact that you can't always win.

GORDON: Well, I want everyone to think that I am a "good guy."

BOB: How far would you go in your efforts to make everyone think that you are a good guy?

GORDON: That's exactly where frustration comes in. You go to any lengths and still you fail.

BILL: I have never been quite satisfied because I have never finished an important undertaking. I find I get tired after a while.

ART: Well, suppose we say there are degrees of frustration. Would not we all agree on that?

FERN: (Turning to the leader.) Are you frustrated now, with our understanding of the concept of ambivalence?

TED B.: Are we picking on you because we are talking too much at our meeting and this is our way out? That is, instead of picking on ourselves for talking too much we are picking on the leader.

TED M.: I just can't seem to listen to content this morning.

CHARLES: I think that's because we find it difficult to work in groups.

BOB: I think we are out of focus now.

ART: Why do we have to live so rigidly by a rule? All of us have led conferences and we know we should not talk so much. If the leader feels like talking sometimes, why shouldn't he, rule or no rule?

At the start of the foregoing exchange the leader challenged Ted M. and the group, rejoining to Ted's challenge of the leader by the statement, "What does the group think?" This was followed by a fruitful analysis of the ambivalent feelings experienced by leaders.

CONSENSUS

Consensus, that is, genuine agreement and likemindedness, is certainly a desirable objective in industrial and business organization. It is healthy in team work if it is reached after honest initial difference. Managers and subordinates, it is to be expected, will not always agree on policy or interpretations or administration of policy. Final agreement may be reached because of fear of the disapproval of a superior or of one's peer group. It isn't always easy to assume responsibility for a minority view or an independent position. An individual or a group that submits because of personal or professional risks or out of boredom is not in agreement. This is false consensus.

Consensus is not arrived at simply through agreeing or not agreeing. Contradictory issues are involved in even simple questions. One may decide to go along with a decision although unconvinced of its logic or practicality. The time factor, costs, insufficient data, a willingness to experiment, these and many other variables may enter into one's agreement to go along despite fundamental disagreement on the principal problem. In a word, a free choice exercised by the participant is the resultant of contradictory views and feelings. The test of genuine consensus is the freedom to agree or not to agree with the manager or group. This is democracy in action in an industrial setting.

In no setting which involves group action, however, is it realistic for anyone always to do, say, or act as he pleases. Every situation, short of chaos, has some structure, organization, and, hence, limits. Any meeting of two or more managers or subordinates which is more than accidental has a purpose more or less defined. The purpose or objectives of the meeting may be structured by company policy or line objectives over which the members of the group have little or no control.

Within the wider objectives of the meeting or conferences the group may be empowered to determine its own procedure, interpretation, or reach its own decisions. The matters over which group decision is in order and the objectives which lie out of its jurisdiction should be clear to all. If the group (or manager) is given responsibility to decide, that decision must be accepted and others in the hierarchy must be bound by it. To grant discretion or authority and then to deny its exercise by those granted such power is to destroy creativity, loyalty, and interest. A manager, who, aware of a predetermined policy, invites his associates to explore the matter to reach a decision is engaging in sheer manipulation or futile talk and breeds mistrust in management.

The average adult working in and through conferences may not always be able to articulate the idea of limits or the inevitability of contradictory assumptions in seeking solutions to problems. Nonetheless he does, most often, recognize the need for compromise which is honest and is usually willing to be partially satisfied and partially dissatisfied provided his differences are respected. One is willing to submerge differences for the sake of a cooperative group if one is aware that he is free not to.

Group meetings or individual conferences cannot be productive if all is sweetness and light. It is out of genuine difference, honestly expressed and sincerely welcomed, that one learns to weigh other points of view, to modify one's own, and to make a contribution to the effectiveness of others.

The foregoing discussion will probably carry more meaning if we cite some discussion on consensus by one of the groups:

CHARLES: The leader should not force us in either direction.

ART: I think consensus is a disguised form of seeking reassurance. You improve morale even though you do not gain the decision you like. That is, you improve upon morale.

TED M.: I think the group members do gain something if there is consensus.

ART: You give way, to try to oblige the members.

TED M.: Yes.

ART: I don't think giving him reassurance helps. Isn't that pseudo-praise?

TED M.: Yes, I think it is helpful.

LEADER: Is consensus sound psychology? Don't we ordinarily settle for less than 100 per cent agreement in most situations?

TED M.: Isn't that what is meant by partialization? It is not a matter of all or nothing.

BOB: I think I understand now what you mean when you write that "people should discover their strength and weaknesses so that they can relate partially satisfied and partially dissatisfied." I think we have to do that all of the time.

LEADER: If all of us agreed that each of us is free to disagree, we are more likely building consensus.

BOB: How can one insist upon agreement? That is a contradiction in terms.

TED M.: You can't insist upon agreement but we might all agree to let people alone.

BOB: I'd like to return to the employee who came in late. Didn't you in effect insist that he be on time at 7:30?

LEADER: Did I insist that he come in on time, or did I insist on the fact that there is a *condition* namely, 7:30 is the starting time? I didn't even insist on that. I simply stated that there was nothing I could do or that he could do about 7:30 being the agreed upon starting time. Aren't there conditions not subject to exploration or qualification? Authority comes from the conditions not from the arbitrary insistence of a superior.

BOB: I think I see the point for the first time. If in group discussion we help the members to see what the realistic conditions are under which they have to operate, instead of the leader insisting, we will make a lot more progress.

LEADER: Are we ready to move on to another topic? (The members did not want to move on, but wanted to continue with this topic.)

ART: I think the fact that you have a structure in the organization means that you have more freedom, but we should also try to point out that rules are not just arbitrary. We have to justify the rule.

LEADER: Would this be an illustration of what you are saying, Art? Suppose 6 o'clock is dinner time in a home, and one of the children says at 5:30, "but I'm hungry now." Is the 6 o'clock rule qualified and is the child permitted to eat?

BOB: I think that depends upon the situation and upon the family. If I were the parent, I'd say wait until 6 o'clock so that your mother doesn't have to do extra work. I think the child will accept what seems to be an irritating rule if the rule seems reasonable.

TED M.: It's like stopping for a red light. I stop although I don't like it because I understand the need for the rule.

The manager who has assimilated the points of view presented here sees new horizons. Becoming a skilled manager no longer appears to be a matter of attending a few conferences or picking up a few "good pointers" here and there. To carry out the function of management, namely, the development of others, requires the development of oneself. The development of self is as broad as one's problems, interests, and efforts. The next chapter deals with some characteristics of a manager who has discovered how to use himself for the development of his subordinates.

NOTES

1. William H. Whyte Jr., *The Organization Man* (New York: Simon and Shuster, 1956).

2. The phrase was suggested by the title, *Learning in a Multidimensional World*, Chapter VIII of *Training for Human Relations* by F. J. Roethlisberger and others (Cambridge, Mass.: Harvard University Press, 1954). This difficult study is rewarding, provocative, and clarifying.

3. The members of the workshop were requested to read my book, *Learning Through Discussion*, before attending the workshop. Reading, of course, is another form of obtaining answers. Readers get no more out of the reading of a volume than they are able to read into and between the lines with reference to their own vital interests. The prior reading of the book is requested in order to structure the problems to be discussed at the workshop. The assumption is made that the readers will possess an initial interest in the topics discussed since they are the kinds of problems confronting managers.

4. Harry Stack Sullivan called this "selective inattention." See Chapter 3 in his *Clinical Studies in Psychiatry*, W. W. Norton and Co. New York, 1956.

VI

CHARACTERISTICS OF A SKILLED MANAGER

O NE of the chief functions of a manager is his responsibility to help the growth of the people whom he manages. Effective help is based upon knowledge of what occurs between people working together and upon an understanding of how to make use of that knowledge in a multidimensional context.

We now present some of the characteristics of the skilled manager. The excerpts will indicate how the leader of the group applied his understanding of the learning process.

The outstanding qualities of a skilled manager are:

1. Refrains from making narrow moral judgments about his associates and subordinates.
2. Keeps his personal needs under control.
3. Recognizes the importance of the learner's feelings.
4. Starts where the learner is.
5. Accepts differences (permissive atmosphere).
6. Recreates himself.

MORAL JUDGMENT VERSUS UNDERSTANDING

PETE: I'd been watching this guy horse around disturbing the whole line. I finally got fed up and yelled to him to cut it out.

What do you suppose happened? Right in front of the whole line he yells, "You know what you can do? You can go straight to hell." Now no one can talk like that to me.

LEADER: He did, though, didn't he?

PETE: But I wouldn't let him get away with that kind of talk to me.

TOM: What did you say to him?

PETE: What do you suppose? I fired him. No supervisor can allow any employee to talk to him that way, especially in front of other workers. And, besides, I couldn't permit my authority to be questioned.

LEADER: I take it, Pete, you were in charge and you couldn't permit one of your workers to bawl you out?

PETE: Exactly. A lot of respect I'd get if that guy got away with that kind of talk.

LEADER: You feel that by firing the chap you retained the respect of other employees who witnessed the scene?

PETE: Well, no one is going to talk that way to me without thinking twice about it.

LEADER: You mean, Pete, they'll be afraid of what would happen if they did?

PETE: Exactly.

LEADER: Do all of you agree that the other employees' respect for Pete was maintained or increased?

TOM: I think they were more afraid of Pete. That isn't respect. That's fear.

PETE: Call it what you want. I had to show who was boss.

LEADER: Someone, Pete, had to control and that was you, the supervisor?

PETE: Certainly. If a supervisor permitted that kind of talk, he'd have no control over anybody.

LEADER: Does anyone want to comment on this? (Silence for about thirty seconds.)

ARTHUR: I've got a feeling there's something different that Pete might have done but I don't know what it is. That's true, isn't it? (Turning to Leader.)

LEADER: I'd like to suggest we role play this situation to try and discover whether Arthur has a point. Any objections? (There was enthusiastic approval.)

Pete volunteered to be the employee, Joe. The leader took the role of the supervisor:[1]

SUPERVISOR: Joe, would you please step into my office before noon? Thanks. (A few minutes later Joe appears in the supervisor's office.)

SUPERVISOR: Sit down, Joe. It was getting pretty hot between us a few minutes ago. Frankly, I was rather upset myself. Something is sure off key to make you feel so badly that you spoke as you did. Perhaps I did something wrong or you did or both of us did. If we talk about it, maybe both of us will feel better about each other. What gives, Joe?

JOE: Well, I feel you've been riding me all week and I'm fed up.

SUPERVISOR: You mean I'm just picking on you because I'm mean and nasty? I certainly don't feel that way toward you, Joe.

JOE: Why is it I'm the one that's bawled out all the time?

SUPERVISOR: You mean I have never tried to help the other operators or that I have not tried to help you?

JOE: Hell, I'm trying to do my job. I do a pretty good job and you know it.

SUPERVISOR: You are doing a good job and I do know it. But all of us can always try to do a better job, I suppose. That's part of my responsibility. Maybe I'm not helping you in the right way?

JOE: Well, I guess I've horsed around more than the others and kind of got under your skin.

SUPERVISOR: I don't take this personally, Joe. I know you must have felt badly because I spoke to you so many times about the line being slowed down but all I was trying to do was to help you see that. I'm sorry you felt that badly.

JOE: I blew my top because I felt you were picking on me. I guess I shouldn't have said what I said and I don't blame you for getting sore.

SUPERVISOR: I'm not sore, Joe. I simply wanted to help you and myself to get this straightened out. Both of us have a job to do and we want to get it done as well as we can.

JOE: Gee, thanks a lot. I guess I had it coming.

SUPERVISOR: I'm not blaming you. All I wanted to do was to try and clear up any bad feeling between us. I'm glad we had this talk. Be seeing you.

The workshop group discussed the role-playing scene:

ARTHUR: I certainly sense something different in the way you (Leader) spoke to Pete but I'm still not able to put it into language.

PETE: I had all the fight taken out of me when I realized the supervisor wasn't picking on me.

LEADER: Just what do you think made the difference?

PETE: I guess you weren't trying to boss me.

LEADER: You mean I wasn't exercising authority?

ARTHUR: Oh yes you were. You called him in and you told him you were responsible for the line operations.

PETE: That's true but I still say he wasn't trying to boss me.

LEADER: Can you put that in a different way, Pete?

PETE: Well, neither one of us had to be right. You were interested in the work and not in bawling me out or showing who was going to be boss.

LEADER: Did I lose your respect by the way I talked to you?

PETE: Of course not. I left feeling a lot more respect for you.

LEADER: I thought you said earlier that if you permitted an employee to talk that way to a supervisor the employees would have no respect for you? You would lose your authority. (Laughter.)

PETE: I see the difference. In the first case they're afraid of you but in your case they really respect you.

The group continued with the discussion. It was pointed out that unless the supervisor realized how the subordinate felt and understood his feelings he would fall into the trap of starting an argument. The supervisor's own need to defend himself would get in the way. The supervisor would have *to condemn* the subordinate to justify his own sense of insecurity because his "authority" was being threatened. If, however, the supervisor realizes his job is to help improve performance, he tries not to make moral judgments about the subordinate but to understand what is taking place and how to improve performance. The company delegates responsibility to the supervisor to manage people in relation to a given task, not to preach to them or to use them as an out for his own hurt feelings. His personal feelings cannot be other than they happen to be, but they can be controlled if the supervisor is clear about his function. No one, especially one who is insecure as a supervisor, relishes being told, in front of others, to go to hell. The supervisor's skill lies precisely in the ability to keep his spontaneous personal reaction to such remarks apart from his professional supervisory function, which is to help those for whom he is responsible. Of course, if, over a period of time and a series of similar incidents, the subordinate cannot be helped, the supervisor must judge whether his services are to be retained by the organization.

Throughout the above discussion the leader at no time made any moral judgment of the reflections of the participants. He tried rather to understand what was being said and to appreciate the feelings being expressed.

THE CONTROL OF PERSONAL NEEDS

A manager, however skilled in his performance, is a person who seeks status, social approval, and power. He wants to be well thought of. Anyone who wields power or authority finds it difficult to resist exercising it for personal needs. Furthermore, the temptation to make use of authority is especially difficult to overcome when one's authority is questioned. Status and self-approval are threatened. To meet the challenge, one is driven to control the challenger, to win over him.

The need to make friends and be popular, to be socially accepted, is as pervasive in our society as is our fear of social disapproval. The need to dominate others is a result of one's lack of self-control. We seek reassurance for felt inadequacies through dominance over others (people or things). Much of our self-disesteem is below the level of direct awareness. We sense, rather than recognize, our inadequacies. To protect ourselves against conscious recognition of attitudes and feelings, we would rather not discover that we build, over the years, a pretty picture of what we would like others to think we are like. This becomes our self-idealized image. When this image is attacked, we feel anxious, tense, and afraid. This is the time to seek reassurance by winning over others or over situations. If we win, we feel reassured, at least momentarily.

Unfortunately one cannot be reassured about something he is not sure of in the first place. Therefore, it becomes necessary to seek reassurance for the reassurance—which really doesn't work. This continues for years. Each of us is kept busy building defenses and justifications for what we are and do and think and believe. We build pretenses, pretending to be what we are not and denying that we are as we are.

The function of a manager is to encourage others to develop through his help. Too often, managers use others as a release for their own tensions. Skirting doubts regarding one's decision or knowledge or control is accompanied by uneasy feelings which may range from momentary irritation to quasi-panic. The temptation to find a target upon which to vent one's dissatisfaction is not easily resisted. The following remarks occurred during the second meeting of a workshop. We were discussing the nature of thinking:

DOUG: Obviously, we think with our mind?
LEADER: And where is the mind?
GORDON: Why in the brain, of course.
DOUG: That's where all ideas come from, the brain.

At this point, I became impatient (dimension of personal need of leader). I had gone through this analysis numerous times with college students and various adult groups. I could easily predict the kinds of arguments which would be presented. Time and again I had experienced the resistance set up to entertaining a radically different conception of the nature of thinking from the traditional notion that ideas are formed in the brain. I felt it might be better to telescope the discussion and save time. (This was my defensive rationalization for wanting to get rid of my mounting irritation. I did not want to recognize that I was losing control. At the time this was happening I was not aware of what was taking place.)

LEADER: Ideas do not come from the brain. They come from the entire body. The entire organism is involved. (I gave some examples of how a child learns the "idea" of h-a-t. It feels the texture, bites it, looks at it, and places it on the head while the mother says, "hat, hat." The child associates the sounds "hat, hat" with feeling it in the fingers and looking at it. The various senses, organs, muscles in eyes and arms, and fingers are tied in with the sound of "hat." The word gradually becomes the symbol for the *bodily* experiences and the idea "hat" is developed.) I wonder if this is clear to all of you?

DOUG: That's what I said in the first place. We think with our mind, our brain.

LEADER: You mean, Doug, that mind and brain are the same?

DOUG: Certainly.

LEADER: I'm afraid I did not make clear what I was trying to convey. Mind is not in the brain. Mind is all over the body. It is what the body does.

DOUG: Well, that's your opinion and I have mine.

LEADER: I beg your pardon. That is not my opinion. That is the conclusion to which the vast majority of physiological psychologists and neurologists have come as a result of a large body of solid evidence. (Doug shrugged his shoulders and remained silent as did the others.)

The reader will probably read into "I beg your pardon" something of the hostility I felt and he will be right. I had become angry, annoyed, and hostile and took it out on Doug. I used him as a target to rid myself of the irritation. He did not speak during the rest of the session. At the close of the session when I called attention to the lack of control,[2] *my* lack of control, Doug smiled and remarked, "I guess we all do that."

LEADER: I wasn't very helpful to you, Doug. I helped myself at your expense. You challenged my authority in front of the group and I felt something of the way Pete felt. I had to save face and I bawled you out in a polite manner. I suppose you felt badly and that's why you clammed up.

Doug: Sure, I felt we were having a fight and I thought, "The hell with him. I'm not going to stick my neck out anymore." But I feel O.K. now.

THE IMPORTANCE OF THE LEARNER'S FEELINGS

Doug's remarks are an apt illustration of how important it is for anyone who wishes to help another to try and understand how the learner feels. I was fairly sure that Doug's silence was the result of my failure, at the time, to appreciate how he felt. My own feelings of annoyance got in the way of my appreciation of his feelings.

Significant change in one's behavior is always accompanied by mixed up feelings. A struggle between the ties of the old and the challenge of the new inevitably arises. More often than not we find it easier to resist changing. This keeps our inner conflict from rising into full consciousness where it can be dealt with openly. Whether reason and logic should play a greater role in learning is not the issue. Feeling is usually the critical factor in significant learning. Anyone charged with the responsibility of helping another to accept a new or modified point of view needs to be convinced of the importance of the learner's feelings. The expression, "Put yourself in another person's shoes" is asserted in theory as often as it is denied in practice.

It is a mistake to believe that most people are convinced by logic or by argument. Argument leads to counter-argument except when neither party to the argument is vitally concerned with what is being discussed. The net result is polite, perfunctory agreement on matters of no particular vital significance. If, however, the learner feels that he is being understood, that no attempt is being made to impose another's will on him, that he is free to accept or reject, in whole or in part, the help of another, that the responsibility for final decision rests solely with him, he is more likely to change. In brief, if the learner feels that he is being understood rather than being criticized, he is more likely to accept the proffered help. The following excerpt is a good illustration of this.

A member of the group raised the question of dealing with chronic lateness of employees. This, of course, is a common problem in industry. Bill was one of the most expert tool makers in the employ of the company. He had been repeatedly late for periods varying from fifteen minutes to an hour and a half. His supervisor, John, who had raised the question, had discussed the matter with Bill on three occasions. Each time Bill promised to be prompt but he continued to arrive late. It was suggested that the group role play the situation. John volunteered to play the role of supervisor and Fred agreed to play the role of Bill. John was asked to leave the meeting for a few minutes in order for the other members of the group to be briefed on the facts.

Fred (Bill) then told us that his wife had had a breakdown and had been institutionalized in a hospital for the mentally unwell. Fred was unable to tell us whether his wife would return in a week or month or year. The doctors were as yet unwilling to make a prognosis. In the meantime, Fred, who was extremely sensitive about his wife's illness, was unable to obtain anyone to take care of his two children. They had to be given their breakfast and sent to school. Fred was trying to manage this every morning. He did not want anyone to know about this misfortune and he did not know what to do.

John was asked to return. He is instructed that he just notices Bill arriving an hour late. This is the eighth time in two weeks:

JOHN: Good morning, Bill. I see you're late again.

BILL: Yeah. I'm sorry but I couldn't help it.

JOHN: I guess you had better step into my office.

BILL: You mean, now?

JOHN: Yep. (They walk to John's office.)

JOHN: What is it this time, Bill? I thought we were all through with your floating in here late.

BILL: I'm sorry. I'm trying my hardest to get here on time but I just can't make it.

JOHN: We've gone all through that before. What in hell's the matter?

BILL: Look, John, we've been through that, too. I told you I had personal reasons for coming in late and that I couldn't talk about it. It's something private and I'd rather not talk about it.

JOHN: See here, Bill. You're one of the best tool makers in this outfit. We want you here. Your work is O.K. But I've got to know why you're coming in late. You aren't entitled to any special privileges unless we know what the trouble is. And if you're bull-headed and don't want my help, you're headed for trouble.

BILL: You mean after fifteen years here I'm gonna be fired?

JOHN: Well, how do you think the other guys feel about your coming in late?

BILL: I do my work and you know it. I'm working faster than any two men in your crew and you know it.

JOHN: That's not the point. If you come in late, others will want the same privilege. Some of the guys have been here more than fifteen years and they report on time.

BILL: Look, I've told you a dozen times that it's something I can't do anything about.

JOHN: Maybe we can. Give me a legitimate reason and maybe we can work something out.

BILL: I'm telling you for the last time I don't want to talk about it.

JOHN: O.K., O.K. If that's the way you want it you can have it. I'm telling you now that if you come in late once more, you're through.

At this point the exchange was halted and the group was asked to evaluate what took place:

GORDON: Well, John was trying to give him all the breaks. He wanted to help Bill but Bill just didn't want his help. John's got his job to do and if Bill refuses to come on time there's nothing John can do except let him go.

JOHN: That's just the way I felt. I want to help the guy and he won't cooperate.

LEADER: That's the way you felt. I wonder how Bill felt?

BILL: I felt trapped and pushed around. I don't think John had any idea how I was feeling although I realized he had his job to do.

GORDON: Then why didn't you tell him what the trouble was?

BILL: Are you starting on me, too? I didn't tell him because I didn't want to.

JOHN: If a guy is bull-headed and won't cooperate, there's nothing anyone can do about it.

LARRY: (To Leader.) Would you have done anything different?

LEADER: Suppose we do this over. Only this time perhaps Fred will take the part of the supervisor and John the part of Bill.

This time Fred took the supervisor's role and John took the role of Bill:

FRED: Hi, John, may I see you in my office for a minute?

JOHN: Sure. (They walk into Fred's office.)

FRED: I guess you must be feeling pretty badly about coming in late again.

JOHN: I sure feel lousy about this, Fred. I promised I'd be on time but it just doesn't work out.

FRED: You know, John, if there's any way I can help, I'd be glad to.

JOHN: There's nothing you can do and I just can't talk about it.

FRED: I know how you must feel. Sometimes we don't like to tell others about our trouble and I can understand that. But it's no go to come in late. It gets around and makes trouble.

At this point neither Fred nor John were able to carry on. The group was stymied:

LEADER: I wonder if any of you can describe the difference between the first and second version of our scene?

LARRY: One thing is clear to me. In the first scene there was a fight, but the second time around there seemed to be more understanding of John.

LEADER: But what happens to John? Is he fired or what?

JOHN: Well, I'll say this much. I didn't feel that Fred was riding me and I felt pretty badly about the spot he was in, too. When I played the role of the supervisor he must have felt I was an S.O.B. In the first case we were both pretty sore at each other. In the second case I felt sorry for Fred, too.

LARRY: How does the matter end, gentlemen?

JOHN: I think maybe I'd tell my supervisor about my wife and see if he had any suggestions.

FRED: Then why didn't you when I asked you what the trouble was?

JOHN: I guess I wasn't sure how you felt about me.

LEADER: How does this strike you? Suppose the supervisor says quietly, "Bill, I've asked you to come in again because I think you should know how I feel about your lateness. I'd be glad to help if I could. You feel you don't want to talk about it and I respect your right to your privacy. I'm sure your reasons for coming late are quite sound. On the other hand, my responsibility is to see that everyone reports on time and I'm sure you will appreciate that. You're a good man and we want very much to keep you here. I think you'll have to make up your own mind what you want to do. I'm very sorry to have to tell you, and you won't like to hear this, I'm sure, that if you are late again, you will have to resign. But I want you to know we'll still be willing to help if you want to share your problem with us. It's entirely up to you. Be seeing you."

The group continued with the discussion. Some felt that I, too, threatened Bill. Unfortunately the written word does not carry the modulation and pitch of voice. Any supervisor who is able to enter into the feelings of an employee who feels put on the spot would not threaten him. His choice of words and manner of speech would spontaneously reflect his understanding of the employee. A closer examination of John's performance (the first version) supports what is being said.

John's first statement sets the argumentative, attacking tone of the meeting. "I see you're late again." Bill wants to know if he is to see him immediately. The answer is not, "If you don't mind" or, "If you please," but a curt, "Yep." Then the condemnatory remark, "What's it this time?" followed by, "I thought we were all through with your *floating* in here late." Follow through John's remarks and in almost each one there is a note of condemnation or aggressiveness. John is not trying to help Bill. John is insistent on bending Bill to his way.

To avoid misunderstanding, let me add that the effort to understand the employee's feelings has nothing to do with "softness" and "pussyfooting." Indeed the most effective way of carrying out one's responsibility is to separate one's personal involvement in being victorious in a dispute from one's carrying out a delegated responsibility. John, the supervisor, is responsible for, among other matters, promptness in reporting for work. An employee repeatedly violates the starting time. John's responsibility is to help the employee arrive on time. He tries to help. Such help is rejected. There may be dozens of reasons, good or real, why an employee rejects help. A skilled manager is keenly aware of this. He understands the poignant complexities in every individual's life. He doesn't argue or browbeat an adult into the pattern he personally would select (maybe). He indicates the objective realities, limitations, and condition of employment and puts it up squarely to the employee to decide what, if anything, *he* wants to do about the situation. Understanding the fear of authority and social disapproval and what they do to one's feelings the least—and the most—the manager can do is to communicate to the employee his appreciation of the fear, anger, hostility, and/or confusion being experienced by the other. Being understood by someone is the first step in growth. If someone fights against us, we tend to fight back. If someone understands how we are fighting with ourselves, we gain strength to continue the inner struggle and do not fight back. It takes two to make a fight.

START WHERE LEARNER IS

The fundamental source of all learning and growth is in the individual. The means for learning and the conditions which aid in learning are found in the situation (including other persons). Unless a person is vitally involved in a problem its resolution can have little or no meaning for him. Other peoples' answers to questions not raised or understood by the learner are unlikely to illuminate his problem.

This helps to explain the inordinate amount of argument between individuals and groups. Each speaker is on a level which is not the same for the hearer. They feel differently and they use words which carry different meanings for each other. The problems and contexts in which they arise are supposedly the same but, in reality, differ. A close observer of family life or a classroom situation can easily recognize the failure of communication between parents and children or teacher and students.

Anyone engaged in helping another to learn must first make certain what the learner's problem is, how he feels about it, what he thinks about it, what, if anything, he would like to do about it. Not taking the learner's attitudes into account can lead to costly failures as the following excerpts show:

NED: Our vice-president gave me the job of developing a training program. We've had no supervisory development in employee relations so I was able to start from scratch.

ANDY: How did you go about it?

NED: I looked around in the journals and handbooks and programs of other companies.

ANDY: You mean you selected a canned program?

NED: Oh, no. I looked over to see what was covered by the field of employee relations and then two of my assistants and myself worked out a program over a long period.

LEADER: And then, Ned?

NED: Well, then we called a meeting of our supervisors and told them about the new program we were undertaking.

LEADER: "*We* were undertaking?" Who is the "we?"

NED: Why the company, of course.

LEADER: Who is the program for?

NED: The supervisors. I thought I said that a moment ago.

LEADER: You gave me the impression it was the company's program.

NED: Sure. It's the company's program for the company's supervisors.

LEADER: I'm not quite sure whether you mean the company wants the program or the supervisors want it?

NED: Oh, I see what you mean. Our vice-president of employee relations made the decision.

DOUG: How old is the program?

At this point I was uncertain whether to interrupt Doug and keep to the issue of whose program it was. Ned certainly did not see what I meant as the subsequent remarks will show. Doug had some other problem in mind. Here is a case where the leader of a group is faced with the inevitable choice of remaining with the problems presented by members who are at different points or dealing with an issue being discussed by one member. Ned was not seeing the problem I had in mind. I decided, therefore, to allow the discussion to go where the group wanted to take it, keeping in mind the need to return to the important issue of "starting where the learner is." I maintained careful attention, waiting for the proper time to return to the theme. The proper time would arrive when Ned and/or a few others found themselves confused enough to recognize that there was a problem they had failed to see:

NED: We started three groups of fifteen each about three months ago.

DOUG: Do you consider it successful?

NED: Frankly, it's too early to judge. But I wouldn't say the supervisors are too happy about it.

LEADER: Could you, perhaps, tell us why?

At this point, the supervisors were not, themselves, vitally concerned with the program. They had not participated in its inception or development or planning. Here was the chance to help the group members meaningfully get into the issue of starting with the learner:

NED: Well, half of them at one time or another don't come to the meetings or they come late and leave before the meeting is over. I'm not blaming them. I know there are many problems and details which require their attention and they're not always free to get away.

ANDY: Do the supervisors say they are learning anything?

NED: They seem interested but keep on complaining that the top boys need the program more than they do.

LEADER: You mean the supervisors feel they do not need the program.

NED: Oh, I'm positive they need the program.

LEADER: Ned, I'm sure of what you think about it. My question was, how do the supervisors feel about it?

NED: As I said, they do seem interested.

LEADER: If they were vitally interested and involved in the program, would they attend regularly, on time, and leave word not to be called out of the meetings except in case of emergency?

FRED: That's for sure.

LEADER: Do you remember our discussion of two days ago about the importance of understanding another person's feelings?

NED: My God. (Ned sat upright and his right hand suddenly covered his mouth.)

LEADER: Yes, Ned?

NED: I'm about ready to resign my job. (There were about ten seconds of dead silence. All were glancing at Ned.) I spend months working on a program which my vice-president tells me he wants and which I tell the supervisors they ought to want. We should never have started any employee relations program without talking with the supervisors to find out their ideas.

LEADER: Finding out about their ideas and. . . .

NED: How they feel.

LEADER: Then how would you build a program?

NED: Obviously by learning what the supervisors thought were their problems.

FRED: Suppose they said they had no employee problems?

NED: Then they wouldn't need a program.

LEADER: But suppose they did say they had no problems. Would you accept that as an accurate statement of fact?

ANDY: Every supervisor has problems every day.

NED: I agree with Andy.

LEADER: I'm sure no one here doubts that. Then what do you do when the supervisors say they have no problem?

NED: (Laughing.) I'd try to find out why they *feel* that way.

LEADER: And thus encourage them to start spilling out some of the difficulties they do run into?

NED: Exactly.

LEADER: Let me ask you a direct question. What's the very first step in starting a development program?

NED: I think I should answer that one. The very first thing to do is to find out how the people who are involved or are going to be involved in it think and feel about it. It is *their* program, not yours.

TED: There is great danger in training directors sitting in the front office thinking up programs.

DOUG: What do you mean?

TED: Our company spent over $250,000 on economic training. It was a promotion fad. Somebody in Chicago had an idea and promoted it. Then some vice-president thought this was an important thing to do. Now our careful follow-up evaluations showed that our supervisors have little interest in the American economic system. They were interested in local plant problems.

Doug: My management asked me why we weren't doing something like your company. We had to get on the bandwagon. I spent four months studying your company's program trying to think up a similar one for ours.

Ted: The overall conclusion after studying the results of our program was that we'll never do anything like it again. If only we had known that first we should have found out how the supervisors felt, we could have saved thousands of dollars spent on useless pamphlets and boring meetings.

When more than one learner is present the problem of starting where the learners are is complicated. Groups can differ in age level, experience, rank, prestige, sex, and size. It becomes physically and psychologically impossible for any one leader to stand by and be close to the thinking and feeling of every individual.

He must judge which of several different issues arising at about the same time is most important in the relevant context. That has to be weighted against the reactions of the member who will be asked to defer to someone else. Will he feel rejected and slighted? Then, too, how many members of a group of ten or fifteen or twenty who see the problem warrant the leader's active participation and challenge? Is it enough if one member raises the relevant point, although the other nine, fourteen, or nineteen are not even intellectually aware of what the problem is?

There are no magical formulae or known rules to be laid down. The professional helper, over a period of time, acquires a sense of timing and discrimination and rapid weighing of the various gains and drawbacks which lead him to the decisions he makes.

The principle of having the point of departure for learning determined by the learner is, nevertheless, sound. Limitations of time and place and of conditions over which neither manager nor learners have control may compel qualification of this principle. Unless the manager realizes that the essential source of development lies within the individual's wanting something and wanting to do something about that wanting he will not understand when and how to qualify the principle.

The fact that no one can transfer one's experience to another is all but impossible to believe. No manager alive, however competent, can transfer his understanding, skill, and executive abilities to another. All the manager (or parent or teacher) can do is to offer help. The learner must possess a need or desire which must be satisfied or expressed by the learner. The manager can *help* to arouse ambition, creativity, or need but only if the learner is free to go forward to use the help.

Often the learner is uninterested in the help. This is when one observes the cardinal error made by the manager. The lack of interest or motivation on the part of the learner is interpreted as a moral matter. Something is "wrong" with him. More often than not the condemnation by the manager is an attempt to buttress his own disesteem. He wasn't able to control, to win, to have his status and superiority acknowledged. He did not succeed, in short, in casting the learner in his image, and feels rejected.

No one can motivate another. The helper can help. The

learner himself decides what to do with the help, when, and how to use it.

THE ACCEPTANCE OF DIFFERENCE

The manager, we have said, can offer help. Offering help is not simple. Helping another on *your* terms is a disguise for helping yourself. A genuine offer of help to another carries with it the acceptance of the other's right to accept or reject the help as he sees fit.

Every individual deals with his experience in his unique way. His uniqueness is his individuality. He is the individual he is because he makes the judgments, carries the responsibilities, and faces the consequences which flow therefrom. Any other view transforms a man into a robot to be manipulated by power seekers and self-appointed gods.

It is almost impossible to communicate through language the meaning of accepting difference in others. The effort must be made, however, since the ability to accept difference in one's associates is, perhaps, the outstanding characteristic of a truly helpful manager.

What is meant by "difference"? No difference exists between individuals if they are indifferent regarding an issue. There is no issue in any meaningful sense unless the parties are both committed to it, unless something vital is at stake for both. One feels the other differs when agreement is sought but not obtained. The basis of love or identification or closeness is mutuality of interest, like-mindedness, sharing. A sharp difference challenges the closeness unless one is able to accept the difference.

Differences bind people together and differences push them

apart. Any parent or married person experiences this fact daily. The stability of married life except in cases where for one reason or another the partners cannot or fear to divorce each other reflects a solid core of identifications which assimilate differences. In short if you like a *person* you like him for better or worse. The popular saying is, "We all have our faults." Who judges what is faulty? The point being made is that we each have our *differences*. Calling it a fault means magnanimous tolerance with its supercilious overtones of self-righteousness (found whenever one "tolerates" another). Viewing it as a difference means an acceptance of the inevitability of no two persons being alike.[3]

To respect a person means to accept him with the splits that both you and he possess. A manager works with people not bookkeepers, boilermakers, statisticians, and staff assistants. People engage in specific tasks. The effective way to help them in their task is to understand them as persons, not to become their taskmaster.

A person is driven, pushed, and pulled by outside influences and by inner tensions, conscious and unconscious. Each of us harbors a jungle through which all kinds of beasts roam, some harmless, some dangerous, and others friendly. Each of us, in his own way, sets up bars to confine the roamings and to prevent "a war of all against each." We set up an involved system of inner defenses to protect us against our split selves. This helps us to cherish the illusion that we are whole, consistent, and in control of ourselves.

A mature adult who "has gained wisdom through affliction schooled" (Aeschylus) is poignantly aware of the complexities involved in even simple decisions. He has become sensative to the rapid oscillations of ambivalent feelings. *He has learned to become comfortable with his own differences.* Realizing his strengths, he does not need to deny his weaknesses to himself or to others. Appreciating his own struggle accompanying learning, the guilt, the hostility, the resistance, the rationalization, and projection, he is able to understand a similar struggle in others. He learns by struggling *with* himself not by avoiding the inner struggle through fighting *against* another. *He learns to leave others alone,* to do what they wish with the help he is professionally obligated to offer. In brief, he learns to accept difference in others. He is sufficiently concerned with the learner as a person to permit him to act as he chooses not as he, the helper, feels he should act.

Here is an excerpt which may make the matter clearer. A group of fifteen had been together for three meetings. There was a general air of confusion. No one understood what the sessions were about. The leader did not appear helpful and had turned aside direct questions which called for intellectual answers:

NED: Look, I asked a simple question. Why can't I get a simple answer?

LEADER: I guess because the answer would be too simple and I'm afraid would not be understood. Perhaps, if we are all a bit more patient the answers will come from you.

FRED: I don't get it, I swear. You're the leader of this group and I think we are entitled to your help.

LEADER: You certainly are, Fred, and I'm trying to help you by *not* giving you direct answers.

NED: (At this point Ned, slowly turning his head left and right, looked at Fred and smiled.)

LEADER: Ned, I think you want to say something.

NED: Yeah, you remind me of another screwball I know. (There was explosive laughter and Ned's face turned red). Oh, you know what I mean, of course.

LEADER: Of course, I do. You mean I remind you of another screwball you know. I can understand that feeling, Ned. Would you like to explain a bit more what you mean?

I was pleased to hear Ned make that remark. He felt free enough after only three meetings to express his genuine feeling about the leader. His feelings were what they were and he had a right to them. Indeed the laughter which followed his remark reflected the release other members received from feelings akin to his. In effect, he was speaking for the group. And why shouldn't they feel this way? Here was a kind of situation which was strange to most of the participants. The expert had no answers, challenged their replies, and created apparent confusion out of what seemed crystal clear.

Ned had the right to think whatever he wished and to differ with the leader even to the point of making what others might judge to be a highly unconventional remark. The leader's obligation was simply to accept Ned's expression as his own sincere feeling.

By way of contrast the reader is asked to recall the incident with Doug, (p. 110). Here the leader failed to accept Doug's difference and blocked his participation for the rest of that session.

To work together in difference requires an uncommon respect for others. It requires, above all, an ability to respect one's own differences from others.

THE RE-CREATION OF SELF

A manager has the responsibility of helping others to develop. The assumption may therefore be made that he possesses or can acquire the skills required to carry out that function. This isn't always the case. Mistakes are made, or pressure and influence can lead to the assumption of responsibility not matched by the necessary competence for the duties. Generally, however, a skilled manager does possess more than average degrees of initiative, drive, competence, and creativity. He understands his job, recognizes how he fits into the company, what the problems are, and the directions he should explore. He possesses confidence in what he is doing and in what should be done.

It is natural in his relations with his associates and subordinates, therefore, that he will express his individuality and his creativity. The problem lies in the forms of expression he seeks for his difference.

The creative manager may try to make others replicas of himself. He seeks to impress himself, his differences, on his associates. He is the boss and, traditionally, the boss issues the orders, although, sometimes they are labeled "requests." I have been present more than once at conferences attended by different echelons in the hierarchy of management. To whom does one turn for official or even informal and unofficial statement of view or policy? The brass sounds off and the tin reverberates. This procedure follows normal expectations.

The manager has a reputation to maintain and a status to preserve. The subordinate has a wife to maintain and a job to preserve. The pattern is set. The subordinate, wanting to get ahead, listens to the manager, learns his ways, and becomes his understudy. The manager, under these circumstances, refers to his subordinate Jones as "doing a good job."

The foregoing, of course, is an exaggerated picture, both too general and too simple. The manager tends to impress his know-how on others whom he is trying to help. His way of helping is being questioned.

An independent, creative person wishes to express himself. A writer produces a play, a poem, a novel. A composer creates an opera, a song, a symphony. An able political organizer fashions a strong party. An imaginative housewife rearranges the home decorations or furniture. In each of these cases the person expresses himself through working on some material. He fashions the material in accord with his own unique design or plan. Generally this is what occurs in management development. The able executive, manager, or supervisor wants to express his ideas by working on people and remaking them according to his design. In this case he is undeniably expressing himself and blocking the development of those whom he is trying to help.

An apparent dilemma arises. The able manager is creative. He has something on the ball. A creative person has to express himself. But if *in the professional* relation of helping others, the helper expresses himself, he prevents the other from expressing himself. The helper ceases to be helpful if he manipulates or uses people for expressing his need to be creative.

Managers of organizations which support management development programs do not want to be known as authoritarian. They pretend to be democratic and permissive. They will agree that managing others, trying to help others, is the core of the manager's job. When asked to describe what they do, however, they do not talk about the subordinates with whom they have spent many meetings trying to communicate about company policy, goals, and their responsibility. They tell about the new products being planned, the capturing of a competitor's market, the new policy in sales. If you persist in asking them about their function in helping subordinates, they complain that it takes too much time, there is too much talk, but "maybe that kind of stuff is important."

William Whyte Jr. devotes a full chapter to *The Executive Ego*.[4] He states that the managers, the true executives, are split. The conflict lies within the work itself.

> If there is one thing that characterizes him, (the executive), it is a fierce desire to control his own destiny and deep down, he resents yielding that control to the Organization, no matter how velvety its grip. He does not want to be done right by; he wants to dominate, not be dominated. . . . He must appear to enjoy listening sympathetically to points of view not his own. He must be less Goal-centered, more employee-centered. It is not enough now that he work hard; he must be a damn good fellow to boot.

Mr. Whyte quotes an executive,

> You've got to endure a tremendous amount of noncontributory labor—this talking back and forth, and meetings, and so on. The emptiness and the frustration of it can be appalling. But you've got to put up with it, there's no mistake about that, and you just hope that you can keep your eye on the contributory phases which put you on the glory road.[5]

What holds true for the executive is generally true for anyone who possesses authority and drive. It is the rare person who measures his real strength by the few occasions he has to use it.

The difficulty lies in failing to distinguish the dual functions of the manager. The use of his technical know-how, his knowledge of specific processes or products, is one thing. His ability to help his associates and subordinates to develop their capacities for the organization is another matter. The manager's need to express himself, his need to assert and control, can be directed to the technical aspects of his performance. His responsibility to develop managers means he must learn to control himself not others.

The creative person in the role of teacher—and that is one of the roles of a manager—remakes, recreates himself. In the very process of working with others whom he is trying to develop[6] the manager will experience his need to control, to tell, to dominate, to win. Realizing that the subordinate must discover insights and answers for himself the manager will feel frustrated, humiliated, confused or irritated over the discovery of poor direction on his part. Or, to turn to another common experience, the learner or learners remain puzzled, cannot find answers, or are at a loss in knowing what to do next. The heavy period of silence ensues. The manager, uncomfortable in and with the silence, then takes over and starts telling or advising. This is followed, in a second or two, by the realization on the manager's part that he fell into his own trap and is taking the ball away from the learner. This realization can lead to self-criticism, greater sensitization, and more effective performance the next time. This is the remaking of oneself. The creative manager, working in the area of developing others, uses himself as the material for expressing himself. This remade product, himself, is placed at the disposal of the learner. The more refined he makes himself, the more effectively will he be able to use himself for the sake of the learner. This remaking of oneself is a never-ceasing process. But while the struggle to improve is never-ending the accompanying satisfaction in sensing improvement and skill is ample reward.

NOTES

1. Ideally, one of the group members should have assumed the role of the supervisor. However, due to the pressure of time, the leader agreed to act as the supervisor, believing that the participants would grasp the difference in attitude that the leader wished to present or catch enough of the difference so that a fruitful discussion would follow.

2. I'd like to share my amusement with the reader over the phrase "the lack of control." No sooner had I written this phrase than I realized that what I felt was *my* lack of control but found myself writing "the" lack of control. This amusing incident reveals the extent of self-defensiveness and our need to justify ourselves.

3. The context here is the *professional* one of manager-learner. The normal marital and family situation cannot escape the moral judgments of its members. In the professional helping situation, however, *understanding difference*, commenting on it but not condemning it, is called for.

4. *Op. cit.*, Chapter 12.

5. *Op. cit.*, p. 151-153.

6. There are other functions of a manager which require his direct independent expression of knowledge, administrative skill, decision and policy making. When he functions as a helper of his associates or subordinates he does not use them as material. He places himself at their disposal. It is in this latter situation where the manager works on himself to remake himself.

VII

THE MANAGER AS LEADER

Managers, as is the case with anyone who wields power, tend to dominate subordinates. Too often they use their power over others to serve their personal needs. One of the chief functions of a manager is to relate to his peer group and subordinates in such a way as to help them carry out the policies of the organization in the most effective manner.

Managers generally possess the particular technological know-how of their job and the responsibility for helping to develop subordinates. The subordinates, therefore, have the right to look to their manager for help in developing their effectiveness for the organizations. This is why there is a manager. He manages people within the limits of company requirements. He helps to develop an *esprit de corps*. He communicates company goals, policies, and needs, and tries to release the creative potential of everyone associated with him. He is there to serve the needs of his subordinates.

His attitude is: "How can I help you? Are there any resources I control which you think may be useful in the more effective performance of your company responsibilities? In what direction do you want help? Are there any problems you face, over which we both share responsibility, which you would like to share with me?"

Or: "Here are some company decisions and policies. I'd like to help you understand why they are in operation although you may not be altogether comfortable with the policies. How do you feel about them?"

The more skilled a manager becomes in interpersonal relations the less threatened and less defensive he becomes. He does not have to win. Job performance has to be improved. If that be the goal, all parties concerned have a contribution to make and that may include a give and take all around. I should like to discuss the way executives seem to handle subordinates and then the manner in which, if they better understood their leadership role, they might relate to their associates.

THE ROOT PROBLEM

It is a truism that business and industrial managers were children. They were under the influence of their parents and the important habits acquired in childhood find expression in their adult conduct. Managers possess prestige, power, and position. This circumstance can easily breed an unholy triple alliance with the limitations a man must live with because of his early childhood experiences.

A developing infant faces a long and difficult struggle in finding his own roots. Normally, he is cuddled by the significant people in his life. This enveloping affection affords a sense of belonging. Soon after the age of two years the child begins to attend more carefully to the spoken word. Greater demands are made upon him. More is expected from him by way of bending to the adult world in which he finds himself. Verbal magic surrounds him. The parents seek to control him in directions he finds uncomfortable and frustrating. The ways through and in which the adults seek to pattern their children furnish the groundwork for many of the undesirable adult ways of handling people. What are the ways parents employ in relating to their children?

There are many kinds of homes and many kinds of parents. Most of the time, in the homes in the United States, the vast majority of parents impose adult patterns upon their young children long before the children are able to comprehend what is being demanded from them. They yield and submit because they need the good will and affection of the significant adults in their lives. Yielding and submission are accompanied by inner (and sometimes outer) hostility, resentment, and, especially, anxiety. Fear of disapproval or the withdrawal of affection is one of the chief weapons of our childhood "education." Parents exercise what is felt by the child as arbitrary authority.

No moral judgment of the parent is being made. The lot of the parent is a difficult one. He is called upon, almost all of the time, to distinguish between MY child and my CHILD. Does the parent really want to help the *child* or does the *parent* want the child to conform to what he, the parent, thinks or feels is necessary? Too often, far too often, the parent wants to and needs to win. He has to control, to reassure himself about felt insecurities. The average adult is a rather insecure person. Not only is our institutional world, in the present time, a terribly complex place, but the tangled webs of daily living in our impersonal loveless surroundings leave us with few vital convictions. All of us seek reassurance. Children are a wonderful target to seek reassurance that we amount to something. We can raise the roof in our own home without fear of recrimination. A man's home is his castle and papa wants to be king even if mama refuses to abdicate as queen. (That's another story.)

The child, as each of us, wants to be like others. He wants to depend upon others. He wants to do what others would like him to do. Call this imitation or, in modern language, identification. At other times, however, the child, as each of us, wants to express his peculiar differences. He wants to assert himself and to be independent. From the earliest times the child learns that being independent carries risks. There is a world of objects and people which block one. Indeed one's own inner world of fear of consequences of individual expression is the greatest block. This is called conscience or, if you like, superego or fear of the boss. If we act too independently, we become scared. We lose the support of those upon whom we depend. If we act too dependently, we are filled with resentment and hostility. We become frustrated at our failure to express our independent self. And so each of us becomes ambivalent, split in our feeling, thinking, and doing.

In the early years the balance is heavily weighted to the side of dependence. No matter how parents try to conceal the fact, much of the time the child is fearful about the demands of the parents. The growing years of preadolescence, adolescence, and postadolescence are filled with anxiety-producing experiences. A great deal of this is inevitable. The late Dr. Harry Stack Sullivan often remarked, "The worst way to bring up children is to provoke anxiety in them. The second worst way is not to produce anxiety."

Each of us, in our contemporary society, carries a considerable load of inferiority feeling. We are basically insecure adults spending a great deal of effort in seeking reassurance, trying to convince ourselves and others that we do amount to something, that we are somebody. We seek outside of ourselves a security which can be found only within ourselves, and which we lack.

Most of us are often out of balance with our environments and with ourselves. We refuse to recognize and accept this fact. We deny it. Without being aware of what takes place, we either conceal, distort, or create attitudes, and engage in the appropriate behavior which justifies our action. We have too much at stake. The pretty pictures we have built up about ourselves must not be spoiled. We incorporate into our own personalities the demands or wishes of others whose approval we seek. If we do this often enough, the demands of others become identified with our "own" desires.

This process, however, is accompanied by resentment at the failure to express our difference and the necessity to conform with what others insist we shall become. We want to be like those around us, so that we may be liked by them, but we want to express our differences so that we might have the feeling of being somebody. If we dare to express our differences, we must be ready to face the disapproval of others. This makes us feel guilty. We become uneasy and afraid of such disapproval. We seek to re-establish ourselves in the good favor of those who disapprove of our conduct. On the other hand, if we succumb to the wishes of others in order to be like them and to win their approval, we feel resentful and hostile at having to suppress our differences.

Were we aware of this polar conflict, we would not be as twisted as many of us are in our thinking and feeling. We are often afraid to be our selves. We deny that we do a lot of faking. We pretend that on the whole, we are consistent, rational, upright, kindly creatures. We conceal from ourselves that we are also, at times, inconsistent, irrational, unrighteous, cruel, hostile, and hateful.

The trouble does not lie in being hostile, cruel, or irrational. That is an inevitable part of our make-up. We *are* that way, at times. *The trouble arises in our denying that we are that way.* It is the self-deception which does not permit us to recognize our conflicting selves. We engage in behavior which, unknown to us, compensates for our inadequacies and shields us from our faults.[1]

USES AND MISUSES OF AUTHORITY

Let us, again, consider Pete's situation, described on p. 104. Pete was not protecting his authority but displaying a lack of authority over himself. He lost control of himself because his own security in relation to his employees was being threatened. He was not sure of himself. Joe's attack increased his anxiety. Pete felt he had to be boss. He needed to control others to reassure himself and quiet his own inchoate feeling of inadequacy. Pete was using Joe as a target for his personal tensions. The members agreed that management expected Pete to help employees improve not to make them whipping boys for personal inadequacies.

Pete is much more likely to win the respect of Joe if he shows Joe his understanding of his feelings. It is rather unlikely that any supervisor who demonstrates such understanding would be exposed to this kind of outburst on the part of an employee. The control is not defined by the *personal* need of the manager to prove to himself that he can dominate and win. The control is limited and defined by the position and *function* delegated to the manager or supervisor. The skilled manager, recognizing this, accepts the feelings of employees. He does not argue about feelings. Through understanding he offers help in defining *the problems*, limits, or responsibilities of the job so that the employee himself may come to feel differently and, hence, react differently. The manager does not exercise control over the employee as a person. He controls *himself* in the carrying out of the functions and responsibilities delegated to him by the organization which employs him. His responsibility is to help the employee to help himself.

If we observe our own behavior closely, we will notice the degree of psychological exploitation of others that we engage in daily. We use other people as sources of our own need gratification. We want them to love us or we wish to control them. Rarely do we accept people on their terms and remain willing to like them and not control them.

When one is emotionally involved with others it becomes difficult to distinguish the willingness to help from the need to control. In a professional relationship, however, the problem is less difficult once it is recognized. As a rule, there is no deep emotional involvement between the manager and his peers and subordinates. The business relationship while friendly is primarily a professional one.

Managers, as most adults, are the products of hit-or-miss development. They are in positions of power using that power to conceal their own disquietude about themselves.[2]

Suppose, for example, a personnel manager describes to the vice-president in charge of personnel a new plan for supervisory participation in company policy. The vice-president, waving his glasses, peremptorily dismisses the suggestion as impractical. It would be all right to hear what the supervisors have to say—*and bring them around to the company's policy* —but the policy of the company stands as the vice-president has determined. The personnel manager reminds his superior that the company has made clear it seeks the active and creative participation of the supervisors. He reminds him of the proclaimed "open door" philosophy described in the last issue of the company's plant magazine, the plea for communication up the line. "We'll do it my way," is the icy rejoinder of the vice-president.

"I'm afraid I simply cannot as a matter of integrity go along with that," the manager replies.

"Well, perhaps, under the circumstances, you had better resign."

"Yes," answers our manager, "that is one alternative. The other is, since I'm convinced that the company will benefit from my plan, that you may want to offer your resignation."

How many personnel managers would have the courage to communicate such real feeling and how many vice-presidents would possess the insight and security to encourage and calmly consider this communication? Yet without this kind of encouragement and insight genuine communication cannot occur.

The power structure of status and position leads to double talk. Face-saving, protection of the idealized image one builds up about oneself, is at stake. Superiors are expected to be superior. It would be a serious letdown to be shown up by a subordinate. The superior must live up to the reputation that his peer group expects and which he accepts. The prestige, esteem, and status accompanying positions of power tend to be self-perpetuating.

All of us, at times, are governed by inadequacies, frustrations, and hostilities which have accumulated over the years. The forms in which these tensions express themselves often remain unrecognized. Sometimes we realize dimly, and too often for our own comfort, that we take it out on others.

Arbitrary authority is not the only method used in educating youngsters. We rely on teaching by definition. We talk endlessly to our children. We tell them what is good and bad for them. It seems as if they pay attention, sometimes. This is largely illusion. The children do attend to the present threat. They learn to yield, to conform, less because they understand adult logic and rationalization but because they quickly and subtly rehearse the consequences of not conforming. Most childhood learning through parental instruction is negative learning. That is, the child builds up a system of security operations. He quickly learns to say and to do that which will avoid getting him into trouble. This kind of general pattern teaches us how to avoid tangling with authority, how to deny our differences, how to cover up anxiety, and how to use words which will not communicate how we really feel. Is it any wonder that adults are so adept in talking their way in or out of anything? We have had years of experience in home and school in concealing genuine feeling.

Telling others almost guarantees that the listener will not learn. All of us have acquired skill in selective inattention. We listen to what we wish to hear and we ignore or pervert what we find uncomfortable to fit in with our present feeling. We hear what we can psychologically afford to hear and we read into what we read what we would like to discover, and not what is there.

Management development generally relies upon the device of telling others what should be done, what is desirable. The learner must create something for himself rather than perfunctorily pay respects (double talk) to the statements of a superior.

Perhaps what we have been trying to communicate will become more clear if we look at the other side of the coin. How can managers function as genuine leaders?

THE MANAGER AS TEACHER

1. *A skilled manager possesses insight into the teaching-learning process.* He recognizes the essential difference between knowledge and understanding. The problem is not one of transferring facts to the learner. The vital issue is to give the learner the chance to translate the data. Knowledge becomes important only when it carries import for its possessor. Possessing knowledge is largely a matter of memory. Being possessed by knowledge is a matter of personal concern. Knowledge that is merely additive is spurious. Genuine learning is the remaking of experience which makes a difference in the behavior of the learner. Ralph Waldo Emerson said this in other words. He declared, "Only so much do I know as I have lived."

A. B. is in charge of the management development program for a nationally known organization. We were talking about the importance of starting where the learner is in trying to help him develop or to change.

A. B. quietly added, "Of course, you can't build any kind of program unless you know what are the problems of the members of the group."

No one commented after his remark. There was a period of silence lasting about twenty seconds. Suddenly A. B. looked up rather startled, and raising both hands to his head, almost shouted, "Oh, no! It suddenly dawns on me that for fifteen years I've been sitting behind my desk writing programs for people I've never seen. How did I know what their problems were? Why, that's terrible! I feel terribly guilty. And I'm supposed to be the expert in management development!"

A. B.'s first statement was a perfunctory repetition of an abstract idea. He was adding to his knowledge. His explosive release was a sudden awareness of the unsound approach he had been making to developing programs. In the second remark the idea we were talking about seeped in and seized him. Somehow he gained insight. He remade his experience. He integrated the idea with past performance and a qualitatively different approach to training appeared.

2. *A skilled executive realizes that significant learning is a function of confusion.* It is only when one does not know answers that learning starts. Is it not obvious that a learner will not seek a meaningful answer unless *he* has a problem? Of course, one may be confused, annoyed, and irritated without learning. But learning must be accompanied by disturbance of some kind. The greater the disturbance or even pain the more likely is it that significant learning can occur.

3. *People fight change and resist learning.* Who of us welcomes annoyance and confusion? It is much less wearisome to justify not changing, to deny the uncertainty and dis-

comfort. The mechanisms we have built to defend our present organization so that we need not change are legion. Rationalizing, lying, projecting, compulsive drinking and eating, sleeping, compulsive card-playing, and talking are a few of our security patterns. The latter is especially noteworthy. Intellectuals, who command the language, can talk themselves into or out of any uncomfortable situation. This is the clue to some of the problems of communication in industry and business.

Who of us has not had the panicky experience of being suddenly asked to see our superior. Our anxiety mounts if we feel especially guilty or insecure about our recent job performance. We enter the office with muscles tightening, swallowing hard, and trying desperately to appear calm and unconcerned. No sooner does our superior raise a question regarding a decision we made than we start defending or justifying our action.

Change the circumstances. We are in casual conversation with a superior. He tells us about a decision he has made and asks us what we think. Often (fortunately not always) if we do not agree, we talk about and around the issue but are substantially saying, "Yes, of course." Too often, we do not feel free to share our fundamental disagreements and speak our piece. The risks are formidable, and we are unwilling to face them.

To recognize responsibility which has not been met, decisions which have been avoided, and errors which have been committed, is to accept feelings of guilt, shame, and lack of esteem. This is not comfortable, and we quickly seek and find ways of disguising, concealing, or distorting the actual situation to save face. Whether one is aware of what takes place or not the fact is that the discomfort is only temporarily resolved. In one way or another it will affect subsequent behavior.

4. *Genuine learning occurs pimarily in an emotional context.* This is not readily appreciated. If an executive vice-president is discussing a financial problem or an instructor is leading a discussion on a problem of distribution, one wonders what the primary emotional context is. The participants are really concerned with their own hidden agenda. What they hear and what they say has to be screened through what they can emotionally afford to accept and to share. The learner, often unknown to himself, makes a rapid survey of the situation. (This is a subtle, short-circuited process). What will the effect of what he says be on him? Will he be approved of or disapproved? Will his reputation for being a smart chap be endangered? What will the other participants' reactions to him be? Promotion is wanted and the mortgage payment is about due. Watch your step!

The director of the management development program of one of our largest corporations stated in his introductory remarks of a three week conference:

"It has been decided that none of the brass will attend these meetings, because we want you to feel free to let your hair down. Toward the close of this conference we'd like to have all of you meet with the president of the company and the vice-presidents and tell us what's on your mind."

The director was naively unaware of the implications of his remarks. He was, in fact, declaring to the participants that communication was blocked between lower and higher echelons and that when they all met he would like to have genuine communication.

A simple test of the emotional context of learning consists in carefully listening to the pitch of voice of the participants. Does the average member of a group speak easily, quietly, inquiringly? Does one sense genuine curiosity in the questioner? Are the *ideas* the vital concern of the speakers? Is it not true, more often than not, that one hears a defensive, argumentative, aggressive, timid, or dominant note in the voice of the participant? Each of us carries our own sense of self-esteem with us all of the time. What we say, do, and feel is subjected to this pervasive need to feel good about ourself. We learn only what, under the circumstances, we can emotionally afford to learn.

5. *The skilled executive realizes that any significant learning is personal.* It is a hard lesson to learn, that no one can transfer one's experience to another. It is difficult enough to learn from one's own experience let alone attempting to transfer one's experience to another individual. We can no more assimilate the insights, feelings, views, or facts of another than we can assimilate the food *they* ingest. All learning is essentially personal. No one can teach another. Motivation must be personal. The teacher can provide the most favorable setting for learning to take place. Whether it will depends on the learner.

6. *The starting point of all teaching or fruitful discussion must be where the learner is, not where the speaker would like him or expects him to be.*

7. *A skillful executive refrains from using the learner for his personal emotional needs.* Who of us can easily deny our

own life? The need to be or appear right is characteristic of every normal person. We want to win, especially if we lose. Most of us carry around quite a mess of inferiority feelings about a great many matters. There has been a tremendous amount of frustration in our early growing periods and in addition, we continue to experience frustration on our jobs, in our personal relations, and in our understanding of the confused and uncertain times. I am not suggesting that most of us require institutional care. I am indicating that each of us carries quite a load of unsolved anxieties and tensions, most of which we are unaware. We exploit others psychologically as a release of some of this unresolved tension. This is especially true of those who find themselves in authoritative status. The authority of position is a terrible temptation, and only the skilled executive has experienced the awful guilt which follows its exercise.

Many executives reach their position through hard work combined with ability. The work and ability revolve around special technical areas which do not necessarily involve relating to or understanding people. Financial and industrial success does not guarantee humility or sensitivity to people.

Those who are by habit and training accustomed to wield power are unlikely to yield it. The shadowy picture others have of them and the idealized image they have built up about themselves cannot easily be exposed to the light of reality.

None of us is quite the fine, consistent, upright creature we believe ourselves to be. But each of us spends a great deal of time and effort in pretending that we are. Over the years we build involved systems of defenses against recognizing our splits, inconsistencies, deep frustrations, and disappointments.

We try to drug, distort, or to deny basic conflicts in our inner life. Some try to achieve relative peace of mind by spending a few dollars for a book or for a bottle.

Others seek reassurance by seeking to bend others to their will. They have to control, to dominate, to win at any costs. People in power have ready targets, their subordinates. This is what we mean by psychological exploitation of others.

The executive who gains insight into his need to dominate and the defensive, protective role it plays in his life is likely to experience guilt and humiliation, and, in time, freer and closer relations with his subordinates. Useful targets can then become helpful associates.

8. *The understanding manager attends to the feelings of the learner and refrains from narrow moral judgments about his performance.* This does not exclude holding the learner responsible for his part in the learning experience. It does exclude name calling and pontifical blame or praise.

9. *The skilled executive challenges the learner.* Challenge does not imply victory for the manager. The participants are challenged not in order to control them but to help them in so far as possible on their terms. The executive stands by and permits the learner to do what he wants with the challenge, even to reject it. The time and place of challenge as well as the sharpness of it depend on the prior relationships built up between subordinate and superior.

Every executive, like each of us, wants to win, and be right. Hence, the insightful executive also challenges himself. He understands his own need to dominate, to control, to be right, to be approved of. A manager who struggles with this problem gains increasing strength and inner security. He learns to be less uncomfortable even when his help is rejected. He feels that he is working with the group and each member; each learner is there *to use him*. The subordinate raises questions, differs, suggests, asks for help, or disagrees. The manager is the resource for the developing subordinate.

10. *Most important, perhaps, is the ability of the executive to accept the differences in the learner*. To free the subordinate to the point where he can afford and dare to be more of his real self, to express, easily and freely, his difference with the authority, is to create the kind of permissive atmosphere which releases the blocked creativity of most learners. There is no fear of disapproval, no threat to self-esteem, no ugly competitiveness, no badgering sarcasm, no wisecracking but a deeply felt sense of mutual respect and common seeking for growth and development.

An executive cannot help creating this kind of atmosphere if he himself possesses genuine self-respect. That inevitably must communicate itself to others. Self-respect, in this context, is born out of one's recognition and realization of the piebald character which all men possess. It stems from understanding the difficulty and confusion which accompanies learning, the resistance to change, the need to be defensive, the need to dominate and control and be right, the need to win.

Listen to a national sales manager trying to discover why sales have dropped in the middle states' division of the company. He is conferring with the divisional sales manager:

What in hell is wrong with this office? Don't your people know their job? Last week X company canceled their order because delivery wasn't made on time. Company Y never got our bid. What's wrong with this outfit, anyway? No one is indispensable, you know.

The national sales manager did not know, at the time, that the divisional sales manager had assumed his new duties only two days before the visit and had not had the opportunity to acquaint himself with the current orders. He was unaware that a clerk in the receiving department of company X had made an error and failed to report the receipt of the order. Had he given the divisional sales manager the opportunity, the national sales manager would have learned that their credit manager had reported company Y had gone into voluntary bankruptcy.

When the facts were made known, the national sales manager gruffly added, "Why don't people tell me these things?" His unjustified attack was buttressed by defensive justification.

A self-respecting manager, of course, would not have permitted himself the luxury of bawling out the district manager. If he had so indulged himself, he would, on discovering the facts, have felt humiliated and would have forthwith communicated his profound regrets over behaving rather badly. Respect for self includes the ready admission of occasional failure, and thus wins the respect and confidence of subordinates. Such understanding leads to a partial resolution of the age old problem, that of tempering power through service to others. By controlling himself, the skilled manager helps his subordinates to develop their own potentialities regarding effective job performance. That is the function of the manager.

The foregoing chapters were intended to reveal the horizon not to detail the topography. There is no one road to manager development and no single cult to which one must swear allegiance. Knowledge of the teaching-learning process is important. The more reliable and valid such knowledge is the more effective will management development be. The multidimensional character of learning, however, cautions us against substituting formulae and rules for sensitivity and skill.

Skill is demonstrated through the *way* one learns and applies learning in changing contexts. Sometimes spontaneity is more important than structured purpose. At other times challenge is called for rather than conformity, understanding rather than rightness, silence rather than utterance. At all times patience is in order. When, how, and under what circumstances the leader makes his judgments no one but the leader can decide. The manager with a warm, helpful spirit can develop this skill through a deepened professional understanding of the learning process.

SELECTED READINGS

The titles listed here have been carefully selected for their importance in illuminating the problems of management development. From different points of view the authors focus on the need for self-discovery and self-realization as the important bases for learning how to help others toward their self-realization.

The reader who feels the need for further study will discover many suggestions for further readings in these volumes.

Argyris, Chris. "Research Trends in Executive Behavior," *Advanced Management*, March 1956.

———, "Top Management Dilemma: Company Needs vs. Individual Development," *Personnel*, September 1955. Both articles are an analysis of the dilemma of executives. The hard-driving, ambitious, aggressive executives are usually *not* the most effective leaders for developing people. Suggestions for resolving this dilemma are made.

Drucker, Peter F. *The Practice of Management*. Harper and Brothers, 1954. An examination of the character of talent required of managers, the nature and structure of management, what is involved in managing a business and managing managers. Material is presented from six of the leading corporations of this country.

May, Rollo. *Man's Search For Himself*, New York: W. W. Norton and Company, 1953. One of the best presentations, without technical jargon, by a well-known clinical psychologist, of how an individual can be helped to gain insight into himself and achieve self-realization.

McGregor, Douglas. "Line Management's Responsibility for Human Relations." *American Management Association, Manufacturing Series* No. 213, 1953.

Roethlisberger, F. J. and others. *Training for Human Relations*, Cambridge, Mass.: Harvard University Press, 1954. This small and difficult study is a wise report on what is involved in learning. The writers analyze the "training" groups' experiences over a period of several years and show something of the frustrations, skepticism, and growth of all concerned.

Sampson, Robert C. *The Staff Role in Management*, New York: Harper and Brothers, 1955. One of the best analyses of the function of staff personnel and their relations to line authority.

Tead, Ordway. *The Art of Administration*, New York: McGraw-Hill Book Co., 1951. A well-known study of the nature of administration and the problems of relating individual personalities to corporate and industrial complexities and contradictions. On another level, Mr. Tead deals with many of the same basic issues discussed in the present volume.

Whyte, William H. Jr. *The Organization Man*, New York: Simon and Schuster, 1956. A well-documented analysis of the dangers of becoming a well-rounded popular guy whose creativity is destroyed in the process. Really, a study of how effective managers *cannot* be developed.

NOTES

1. N. Cantor, *Dynamics of Learning* (3rd. Ed.; Buffalo: Henry Stewart, Inc., 1956).

2. The danger of overgeneralization is always present. I ask the reader's indulgence. The words used should not trap the reader in missing what I mean. Of course, there are all kinds of managerial personnel. There are many sensitive, cooperative executives seeking to help their associates. Each has a different threshold of frustration. Some can take more, some less. I have found more understanding in lower management. I hope I'll not be considered cynical if I remark that having less power they push people around less often.